KT-582-527

Branding

Stephen Coomber

MARKETING

04.08

■ *The* fast track route to mastering brands and branding

■ Covers the key areas of branding, from developing a strong brand personality and differentiation to brand valuation and protecting your brand

■ Examples and lessons from some of the world's most successful businesses, including CocaCola, Intel, Toyota and Virgin, and ideas from the smartest thinkers, including David Aaker, Philip Kotler, John Quelch, Al Ries and Ted Levitt

■ Includes a glossary of key concepts and a comprehensive resources guide

>>EXPRESS EXEC.COM<<
essential management thinking at your fingertips

Copyright © Capstone Publishing 2002

The right of Stephen Coomber to be identified as the author of this work has been asserted in accordance with the Copyright, Designs and Patents Act 1988

First published 2002 by
Capstone Publishing (A Wiley Company)
8 Newtec Place
Magdalen Road
Oxford OX4 1RE
United Kingdom
http://www.capstoneideas.com

CIP catalogue records for this book are available from the British Library and the US Library of Congress

ISBN 1-84112-410-9

Printed and bound in Great Britain

This book is printed on acid-free paper

Contents

Introduction to ExpressExec

ExpressExec is 3 million words of the latest management thinking compiled into 10 modules. Each module contains 10 individual titles forming a comprehensive resource of current business practice written by leading practitioners in their field. From brand management to balanced scorecard, ExpressExec enables you to grasp the key concepts behind each subject and implement the theory immediately. Each of the 100 titles is available in print and electronic formats.

Through the ExpressExec.com Website you will discover that you can access the complete resource in a number of ways:

» printed books or e-books;
» e-content – PDF or XML (for licensed syndication) adding value to an intranet or Internet site;
» a corporate e-learning/knowledge management solution providing a cost-effective platform for developing skills and sharing knowledge within an organization;
» bespoke delivery – tailored solutions to solve your need.

Why not visit www.expressexec.com and register for free key management briefings, a monthly newsletter and interactive skills checklists. Share your ideas about ExpressExec and your thoughts about business today.

Please contact elound@wiley-capstone.co.uk for more information.

Introduction to Branding

What is the role of branding in the modern world of business? This chapter considers the changing nature of branding, including:

» current debate about the role of brands;
» the world's most valuable brands.

"Brand loyalty is very much like an onion. It has layers and a core.
The core is the user who will stick with you until the very end."
Edwin Artzt, CEO of Procter & Gamble

Branding is not a static discipline. The place it occupies in business
life is constantly being debated and refined. It has gone through, and
continues to go through, periodic reinterpretations and innovations.
At present, it is the advent of the Internet that is exercising the minds
of academics and branding experts. In December 2000, for example,
Regis McKenna, who has been described as one of the fathers of
modern marketing, observed: "Brand has absolutely no hold on the
loyalty of a customer."[1] This is not the kind of statement companies
like to hear, given the marketing budgets spent on brand building and
the reputation of McKenna for successfully predicting future marketing
trends. But reports of the demise of the brand seem greatly exaggerated.
For once, McKenna is in a minority of one.

The debate about the future direction of brands is likely to rumble
on (much as it always has), but, for the thousands of practicing brand
managers and other businesspeople around the globe, that brands have
a future has never been in serious doubt. The fact is that although
brand management goes through periodic reappraisal, and the theory
and the tools that are used to create and sustain a brand alter over time,
brands remain an ever-present part of our lives.

Brands have been called "the shimmering symbols of the modern
age" by the *Financial Times*. Not only has the world of brands expanded
to take in virtually everything that can be made, provided or breathed,
it has re-invented traditional relationships. Small, locally available products have been converted into nationally and internationally renowned
money-earners. A staggering 150 million Unilever products are sold
every single day; over 1.2 billion people use a Gillette product every
day; and 38 million people will eat at a McDonald's restaurant today.

Brands are powerful weapons. They can change the entire landscape
of industries. Some even force themselves deep into the psyche of
entire nations. Vegemite is an Australian cultural icon, as essential to
the rearing of young Australians as their mother's milk. The Italian
love affair with Nutella is a similarly curious phenomenon – and one
likely to keep psychologists at work for many years to come. Nutella's

maker, Ferrero, enigmatically describes its product as "the physical sublimation of chocolate."

The continuing importance of brands is evident from the valuation placed on them. Take the Interbrand survey of brand values in 2000. The remarkable feature is not that brands have lost their significance or allure – far from it, in fact – but that the company that sits at the top of the rankings was founded over one hundred years ago, has extended its brand very little, and makes a large proportion of its profits from a single and largely undifferentiated product.

Table 1.1   The world's most valuable brands, 2000.

Brand	Brand value ($bn)
Coca-Cola	72.53
Microsoft	70.19
IBM	53.19
Intel	39.05
Nokia	38.53
GE	38.13
Ford	36.37
Disney	33.55
McDonald's	27.86
AT&T	25.55

Source: Interbrand

That company is of course Coca-Cola, which at the last count was selling 12,000 products every second across the globe.[2] And, despite having what the company would consider a difficult trading period with a new CEO, Douglas Daft, taking the helm, the Coca-Cola brand was worth $72,537 bn.[3] Coca-Cola is living proof of the power of brands in the modern world.

The annual Interbrand rankings generally reflect economic and business trends. Traditionally the companies that head the rankings (see Table 1.1) are leaders in their markets and have long-established brands. They include familiar names such as General Electric, Ford, Disney, AT&T, Marlboro, and Gillette. In the last decade or so these incumbents have been joined by the hi-tech brigade: Microsoft, IBM, Intel, and Nokia. And in the 2000 rankings the dot-coms continued their climb up the brands value ladder with Yahoo! (#38) and Amazon (#48) leading the branding brat pack. Yahoo!'s brand value grew from $1761 mn in the 1999 Interbrand survey to $6000 mn in 2000, a staggering 258% increase. Amazon's rise was an equally impressive 233% from a value of $1361 mn to $4521 mn.

Judging by the values attributed to the brands appearing in the Interbrand rankings, the role of the brand in marketing strategy seems anything but dead. In fact, brands are everywhere. Omnipresent, ubiquitous, they pervade our lives. They stare at us from the billboards that sit incongruously alongside the cows in fields visible on the daily commute. In cities, ads cover every available space, plastering urban concrete like modern-day frescoes. Japanese teenagers wear electronic billboards on their backs. We wake up in our branded pajamas, brush our teeth with branded toothpaste, eat our branded cereal, and drive to work in our branded automobile. After work we drop into a branded bar to have a glass of our favorite branded drink, then grab some branded fast food before driving home. No doubt you have already substituted the word "branded" with your own personal preferences. That's the power of brands.

Brands, then, at least as far as the business world is concerned, are essential. What is changing, however, is the theory of branding and brands strategy. Part art, part science, branding is the business equivalent of alchemy, with the marketer, brand manager, CEO, and even the humble individual playing the role of alchemist. Base products are branded gold.

The last decade or so has witnessed several important developments in branding: the shifting of responsibility for brands within the organization; the rise and possible fall of the global one-brand-for-the-world concept; the Internet brand; the corporate brand; the personal brand; and not forgetting the appearance of a brand's value as an asset on the balance sheet.

As noted above, branding theory is constantly evolving, as companies try to maintain a competitive edge. Understanding branding, with its rapid pace of change, is like trying to make a living as a session musician: the best you can hope for is to:

» grasp the fundamentals – learn to sing or play an instrument;
» keep up with the latest trends, be they hip-hop, garage, or Latin breakbeat;
» find out contact details for the recording studios in the locality;
» practice like crazy.

Branding is designed to remove the mystique associated with branding theory; identify the key concepts and thinkers; detail the latest trends; show how the great brands do it; list the best branding resources; and finally show how to put it all into practice.

As David Ogilvy, the advertising guru, once said: "Any damn fool can put on a deal, but it takes genius, faith, and perseverance to create a brand."

NOTES

1 "The End of Marketing." *Business 2.0* (UK Edition), December 2000.
2 Coca-Cola corporate material on the Internet at: heritage.coca-cola.com/The_Story_of_Coca-Cola.pdf, sourced in January 2001.
3 *The World's Most Valuable Brands 2000 Survey*. The Interbrand Group. On the Internet at: 63.111.41.5/interbrand/test/html/events/table_1.html and www.eterra.com.ar/Informe_Interbrand_2000.htm

Definition of Terms:

What is a Brand?

Most people can name examples of brands, but the precise meaning of the concept is more difficult. This chapter examines some of the classic definitions of brand. It includes:

» the common characteristics brands share;
» types of brand.

"Today brands are everything, and all kinds of products and services – from accounting firms to sneaker makers to restaurants – are figuring out how to transcend the narrow boundaries of their categories and become a brand surrounded by a Tommy Hilfiger-like buzz."

Tom Peters, business commentator

Branding is a complex, and some might say vague and imprecise, subject. It has its own lexicon of terminology, impenetrable to most non-marketers. Brand systems, brand equity, brand valuation, brand extension: these are all terms associated with the theory of branding. However, before we can begin to understand these concepts we need to pin down that elusive notion of the brand itself. This is not an easy task.

When the McKenna Group, the firm of the celebrated "father of hi-tech marketing", Regis McKenna, conducted a survey of 100 CEOs, the results were a little surprising – and made alarming reading for brand managers everywhere. The CEOs, many of whom were leaders of hi-tech companies in the driving seat of the new economy, were asked, "What is a brand?". To this one question they gave 100 different answers – and therein lies the dilemma.

The unpleasant truth is that there is no pat answer, no single killing definition of a brand. A legal definition might approximate to "a sign that distinguishes the goods of a company from those of another while guaranteeing its origins." But a brand is much more than its dry legal definition. A brand has many different attributes, and the importance and nature of those attributes changes according to whom you ask and when you ask them. The best that can be hoped for is an understanding of what some of the leading thinkers and practitioners have said about brands.

DEFINING BRANDS

As with most management practices, the theory of brands and branding has evolved, and along the way our notion of what constitutes a brand has changed with the times, usually slowly and subtly. In the beginning came the product. Branding was a mark on the product – a signature or symbol – signifying its origin or ownership. The traditional view of what constitutes a brand is summed up by marketing guru Philip Kotler in his classic textbook *Marketing Management*. Kotler writes: "[A brand name is] a name, term, sign, symbol or design, or a combination of these, which is intended to identify the goods or services of one group of sellers and differentiate them from those of competitors."[1]

The trouble with older definitions of brands, such as Kotler's, is that they remain preoccupied with the physical product. The product stands alone; the brand exists within the corporate ether. The product comes first and the brand does little more than make it clear which company made the product and where. John Pemberton's brain tonic is the product, but the brand – Coca-Cola – is much more.

A more recent definition comes from Richard Koch in his book *The Dictionary of Financial Management*. Koch defines a brand as: "A visual design and/or name that is given to a product or service by an organization in order to differentiate it from competing products and which assures consumers that the product will be of high and consistent quality."[2] Reflecting the emphasis of our times, Koch stresses differentiation – making your product or service different (or seem to be different) – and achieving consistent quality.

More recently, and perhaps more usefully, three American consultants have defined branding as "creating a mutually acknowledged relationship between the supplier and buyer that transcends isolated transactions or specific individuals." It is a significant sign of our times that the brand is now pinned around a relationship rather than a product.[3]

Leslie de Chernatony, Professor of Brand Marketing at the UK's Open University Business School, echoes this perception of brands: "The brand is, through the staff, an active participant in any relationship, be it between customer and brand, employee and employee, employee and customer or employee and other stakeholders ... Inadequate communication of the corporation's values and individual's roles in delivering them can quickly result in inconsistencies between the brand's espoused values and the values perceived by stakeholders when dealing with staff."[4]

Perhaps the most practical and contemporary definition of brands comes from the consultants Booz-Allen & Hamilton: "Brands are a shorthand way of communicating critical data to the market to influence decisions. Across a multitude of consumer-focused industries, brands are an important means for differentiation and competitive advantage, although they are most influential when customers lack the data to make informed product choices and/or when the differentiation between competitors' versions of the same product are small to non-existent. Additionally, brands take on more significance when consumers place great importance on the decision being made."[5]

BRAND TYPES

Lynn Upshaw of brand consultants Upshaw & Associates has identified six types of brand, each with its own marketing role.

» **Product brands**, e.g. packaged goods. These are what most people think of when they think of a "brand". They are the original and still the most common type of branded goods – Mercedes cars, Mars bars, and Pepsi-Cola are all examples of product brands.
» **Service brands**, e.g. intangible services. Less common than their product counterparts, service brands are those where the brand is predominantly perceived through the service that is associated with it rather than through the material things to which the brand symbols are attached. Virgin Airlines is a service brand in essence: you purchase the service – air travel Virgin-style from A to B. Fed-Ex, Visa, and Citibank are all service brands.
» **Personal brands**, e.g. the individual as a brand. This probably started with the Hollywood icons of yesteryear – Clark Gable, Marilyn Monroe, even as far back as Charlie Chaplin. Today personal brands encompass a range of personalities, from sports stars – Michael Jordan, Zinedine Zidane, Michael Johnson – through pop music – The Beatles, The Grateful Dead, Britney Spears – to business gurus such as Tony Robbins and Tom Peters.
» **Organizational brands**, e.g. the corporate brands, charities, political parties. Increasingly, the brand transcends the

product/service and is subsumed into the organization. The organization is the brand and the brand becomes an integral part of the strategic planning process. Microsoft, Virgin, and Sony, for example, have all taken the concept of the brand to the core of the corporation.

» **Event brands**, e.g. concerts, tournaments, races. These are events, usually in sports or the arts, that have taken on lives of their own and are promoted as stand-alone brands. The Superbowl, the Olympics, the Three Tenors, and the US Masters are all good examples.

» **Geographical brands**, e.g. countries, cities, resorts. The growth of the tourism and leisure industries and world travel in general has provoked the branding of locations. Ski in the Portes de Soleil, sunbathe on the French Riviera – wherever you take your vacation, it's hard to escape branding.

Another way of looking at brands is to examine some of the common characteristics of the most successful brands. These best-of-breed brands tend to be:

» universal;
» psychological as well as physical;
» able to re-invent themselves;
» global;
» informative;
» handled with care;
» true to themselves.

Universal

The modern world of brands extends to all industries, all businesses. It doesn't matter what business you are in, branding is important. Once the world of brands was dominated by fast-moving consumer goods. Now it is filled with retailers – from Benetton to Wal-Mart – and financial services companies. They realize that branding can provide competitive advantage, no matter whether you sell hot-dogs or provide cleaning services.

Psychological as well as physical

In this new era, brands are driven by consumers. They are psychological as well as physical. Brands are about hearts and minds. "A brand is a promise, and, in the end, you have to keep your promises. A product is the artifact of the truth of a promise. Coke promises refreshment; Gateway Computer promises to be your wagon master across the Silicon prairie. There is no difference between what you sell and what you believe," says futurist Watts Wacker. Selling is believing. More importantly, people buy what they trust and believe in, and are prepared to pay a premium price for it. In the end, branding works because belief sells.

Able to re-invent themselves

The most powerful brands have the power to re-invent businesses, and sometimes entire industries. Take Absolut vodka, for example. Owned by the Swedish state, Absolut is a testament to how powerful branding can be. Ten years ago, the brand was virtually unknown, its product unfashionable, its market dominated by long-established brands. Smirnoff ruled the roost. No longer.

Absolut has emerged from nowhere as the vodka brand of our day. Today it is the fifth largest spirits brand in the world and is present in some 125 markets. In 1999, 60 million liters of Absolut Vodka were sold. Absolut is now the number one imported vodka in the United States, with approximately 60% of the market. In 1999, some 40 million liters were sold in the US alone.

Absolut's success has been built on brilliant brand development. A clever ad campaign has established Absolut as a brand for its times. Ironic and sophisticated, the ads (developed by TBWA Chiat/Day) with their variations on the Absolut bottle, have become classics – so much so that a book of the ads sold a staggering total of more than 150,000 copies. A book about the company is subtitled "the story of a bottle."

Global

Globalization is one of the great rallying cries of our times. Nowhere is it louder than in the world of brands. Global brands are, of course, more easily proclaimed than achieved. Combining global and local elements is a minefield, nowhere more so than in Europe, where cultural and regional differences abound. Market research company Mintel found that 22% of French people are likely to sample a product if it is endorsed by a celebrity. The British, however, remain studiously unimpressed – only 1% said they would be influenced.

It is not only national tastes and preoccupations that the brand must play to. Approaches may differ according to a brand's place and standing in the marketplaces in individual countries. The soft drink Orangina is positioned and priced differently in various countries. It is a global brand that is highly responsive to local markets. In France, for example, it is very popular – the second most purchased soft drink, after Coke – while in the UK it competes as a premium brand in the orange carbonated soft-drink market against local brands such as Tango or Sunkist.

Informative

At its simplest, branding is a statement of ownership. Branding can be traced back to trademarks placed on Greek pots in the seventh century BC and, later, to medieval tradesmen who put trademarks on their products to protect themselves and buyers against inferior imitations. Today, however, brands are a ready source of information as well as identification. As an editorial in *The Economist* acutely observed:[6]

> "The point of brands is, and always has been, to provide information. The form of that information varies from market to market and from time to time. Some products make a visible statement about their users' style, modernity or wealth – examples include clothes, cars and accessories. Others purport to convey reliability, say, or familiarity, or something else. Whatever the information, however, the right question to ask is this: does the buyer still need or want it?"

Handled with care

At one time, brands were unhappily and inaccurately associated with the hard-selling, entrepreneurial superficiality of the 1980s, when deals were everything and brands changed hands as readily as stolen watches in a downtown bar. Conglomerates owned portfolios of brands and managed them to maximize market share. Often, the spirit of the brand – its uniqueness – was lost in the process. There is a paradox here. The lesson that companies learned the hard way is that although brands can be cynically manipulated for profit in the short run, to remain strong over time they require periodic injections of freshness. Brands have to be reborn or they will die; change them too much and you slay the golden goose.

In recent years, brands have been brought back to earth. Companies appreciate that brands are neither frivolous nor a necessary evil, but are important, expensive, and potentially lucrative investments. That they are all-embracing is a fact of life, caused in part by the human needs for re-assurance, labeling, and ease of identity.

True to themselves

The essence of a great brand is that it stays true to the spirit of the thing that it represents. Stray from that truth too far and the consumer will see through the brand. When Bic extended its brand – cheap, easygoing, simple – from practical products such as the ballpoint to the disposable razor and disposable lighter, it worked. Perfume, however, was a step outside the brand's halo.

The great brands stay focused on what made them great in the first place. "Consider Walt Disney," say James Collins and Jerry Porras, the authors of *Built To Last*. "It was his belief that he and his company were about making people happy. If he had thought his business and the brand was about making cartoons, then we would not have Disneyland, Epcot, or the Mighty Ducks hockey team."[7]

Brands, then, are many things to many people. They are prompts, symbols, and representations – activities that have been used since we started buying and selling things. Brands are marketing shorthand that companies hope will lead us to purchase their particular products. Above all, brands represent the added value between one company, product, or service and another. They are an intangible, abstract perception in the mind of the consumer.

LEARNING POINTS

Brand types:

» Product
» Service
» Personal
» Organizational
» Event
» Geographical.

Common characteristics of successful brands:

» Universal
» Physical and psychological
» Re-invent themselves
» Global
» Informative
» Handled with care
» True to themselves.

NOTES

1 Kotler, Philip (1993) *Marketing Management: Analysis, Planning and Control*, 8th edn. Prentice Hall, Engelwood Cliffs, NJ.
2 Koch, Richard (1994) *The Financial Times Guide to Management and Finance*. Financial Times/Pitman Publishing, London.
3 Hill, Sam I., McGrath, Jack, & Dayal, Sandeep (1998) "How to brand sand." *Strategy & Business*, 2nd quarter.
4 *Marketing Business*, May 1999.
5 Totonis, Harry, & Acito, Chris (1998) "Branding the bank: the next source of competitive advantage", *Insights* Newsletter series, Vol **3**, No 1 (March). Booz-Allen & Hamilton, McLean, VA.
6 "Don't get left on the shelf." *The Economist*, July 2,1994.
7 Collins, James C. & Porras, Jerry I. (1998) *Built To Last: Successful Habits of Visionary Companies*, new edn. HarperBusiness, New York.

The Evolution of Brands

The modern idea of a brand has its roots in ancient history. This chapter examines how the concept of the brand has evolved. It includes:

» the introduction of the classical concept of the "product brand";
» where we are now in the evolution of branding.

"A brand is a promise, and, in the end, you have to keep your promises. A product is the artifact of the truth of a promise. Coke promises refreshment; Gateway Computer promises to be your wagon master across the Silicon prairie. There is no difference between what you sell and what you believe."

Watts Wacker, futurist

With the torrent of words devoted to the role of brands in the new economy, and the eulogizing of the astute marketing and branding campaigns of dot-com giants such as Yahoo! and Amazon, many would be forgiven for thinking that the concept of branding is a relatively recent invention. The origins of branding, however, are to be found much further back in history than the advent of e-tailing or the invention of the microchip – further back even than the snake-oil salesmen who roamed the US in the late nineteenth century and who might reasonably be considered the forefathers of modern brand marketers.

In fact, the roots of branding, or of the word at least, stretch as far back as those archetypes of looting and pillaging, the Vikings. In order to understand the role of branding in the business world today, it is essential to get some idea of branding in its historical context. We need to get an idea of how a simple symbol of the possession of a chattel has evolved into an intangible, immaterial, corporate asset worth in some cases billions of dollars.

SETTING THE SCENE

Supposedly Nordic in origin, the word *brand* started life as a noun but has gradually transformed into a verb. (This is an agreeably concise summation of the history of branding.) It is thought that Viking ship-builders branded the boats they built. Branding was also used from early times to mark cattle in order to assert ownership. This use of a brand was akin to what we would now call a trademark. However, it soon became more than just a symbol of ownership. It is not hard to imagine how purchasers of cattle eventually came to rely on the brand as an assurance of quality, and how the brand might have conveyed the cattle owner's reputation and attributes – wealth and power, for example. In this exchange, the brand had taken on the role of adding value – something that is equally true of brands today.

By medieval times a merchant's reputation and the goodwill of satisfied consumers had assumed a function similar to that of brands, assuring product quality just as well-known brands do today. The Vatican even took the step of acknowledging two forms of intellectual property: one, the product and its design; the other, the reputation of the manufacturer or vendor of the product. The Vatican then went further, setting up two courts to deal with issues arising from these forms of intellectual property. A secular court was convened to deal with disputes arising over trademark issues related to the product or its design. And, giving weight to the value placed on reputation by the Vatican, the Church reserved for itself the right to deal with the slander of a reputation. To slander someone's business reputation was considered a sin.

This acknowledgment of the importance of the tradesman's reputation presaged an important development in the evolution of brands. The Vatican tacitly allowed that a value could be placed on an intangible quality such as reputation. This decision was echoed in the late 1980s when the notional value of brands was finally reflected in the balance sheet as an asset. This practice arose in Europe, home of the Vikings, rather than in the United States where so many of the other significant developments in the evolution of branding occurred.

To a considerable extent, the history of brands is tied up with the history of the United States. That the iconic brands of our times are predominately American owes a great deal to the fact that American businesses have continually developed brands at a faster pace than have their European counterparts. This can partly be attributed to geography. American companies had (and have) a huge homogenous national market; European companies do not. While American companies could launch massive advertising and marketing campaigns across the US and the English-speaking world, European companies learned to adapt (or not) to the cultural nuances of individual countries.

THE SNAKE-OIL SALESMEN

In the late nineteenth century, trailers traveled the American countryside laden with every possible known cure, stimulant, medicine, or treatment. The medicine jamborees may have had an indifferent medical record, but their contribution to the success of brands cannot be overlooked. They played a small but significant part in the development of national branding at that time. Patent medicines and tobacco set the trend. Although distributed only regionally, they developed recognizable brand names and identities.

The increased prevalence of brands regionally provided the foundation for growth on a much greater scale. Instead of being restricted to low-quality, regionally distributed products, brands took the great leap forward into the high-quality mass market. The conditions were fertile. Efficient countrywide transportation emerged, so that a successful product made in Chicago could be sold in St Louis cost-effectively.

But improvements were not limited to transport; production processes and packaging improved and advertising became almost respectable. There were also changes in trademark laws, and increasing industrialization and urbanization. While the brands expanded, their management remained resolutely set in its ways. Company owners and directors took responsibility. The array of tools at their disposal – from premiums and free samples to mass advertising – grew quickly.

BETWEEN THE WARS

The period after World War I cemented the place of brands. Advertising became increasingly prevalent and the acquisition of brands became identified with success and development. Consumers wanted Fords, not motor cars; they bought from Sears rather than from elsewhere.

Success brought complexity. Companies began to own a number of brands, which they were able to produce, distribute, and sell *en masse*. Complexity encouraged the functional division of labor, through production lines with workers performing repetitive tasks on a mammoth scale. It also encouraged the functional division of management, which became separated into different functions such as marketing, sales, R&D, and production. The separation was ruthlessly enforced. "It is not necessary for any one department to know what any other department is doing," Henry Ford propounded. "It is the business of those who plan the entire work to see that all of the departments are working … towards the same end." Ford believed that managers should work in isolation, unencumbered by the problems of their colleagues, simply concentrating on what they were employed to do.

The downside of such scientific management is now well known and accepted. Ruthlessly satirized by Charlie Chaplin in *Modern Times*, such science brought with it worker alienation, a lack of co-ordination between different functions, and a complete absence of flexibility. Any sense of individual responsibility was sucked away by the system. Imaginations were never stretched; intelligence was not developed.

While scientific management took management up a lengthy blind alley, brands developed in a new direction. The great proponent of functionalized mass production, Henry Ford, fell from a position of almost total domination thanks to the more innovative management of brands at General Motors.

In 1920 Ford was making a car a minute and the famously black Model T accounted for 60% of the market. General Motors managed to scrimp and scrap its way to around 12%. With Ford cornering the mass market, the accepted wisdom was that the only alternative for competitors lay in the negligibly sized luxury market. GM chief Alfred P. Sloan thought otherwise and concentrated GM's attentions on the middle market, which did not exist as yet. His aim was a car for "every purse and every purpose."

At the time, GM was an unwieldy combination of companies, with eight models which basically competed against each other as well as against Ford. Sloan cut the eight down to five and decided that, rather than competing with each other, each model – an individual brand – would be targeted at a particular segment of the market. The five GM brands – Chevrolet, Oldsmobile, Pontiac, Buick, and Cadillac – were to be updated and changed regularly, and came in more than one color. Ford continued to offer functional, reliable cars: GM offered choice. By 1925, with its new organization and commitment to annual changes in its models, GM had overtaken Ford, which continued to persist with its faithful old Model T. GM made brands work. "Back then, if you said the word 'Pontiac', any consumer in the country could tell you what kind of person drove it," said *BusinessWeek*.[1]

While Sloan at GM proved the importance of brands, in 1931 Procter & Gamble took functional organization a stage further when it created a new function: brand management. With brands such as Ivory and Camay bath soaps, P&G believed that the best way to organize itself would be to give brand responsibility to a single individual: a brand manager. (And you can't argue with P&G's development since: its revenues are now near $40 bn.)

SOCIAL ASPIRATION

The P&G system did not transform the world overnight, but gradually brand management became an accepted functional activity, an adjunct to sales and marketing – often a fairly junior adjunct, at that. Its popularity was fuelled by the economic boom of the 1950s, which brought a profusion of new products and brands. These were supplemented by developments such as shopping centers and the emergence of television advertising. We had never had it so good and had never had so much. Brand management provided some hope of order amid the confusion introduced by prosperity.

By 1967, 84% of large manufacturers of consumer packaged goods in the United States had brand managers. Though titles have changed, this system largely prevails today.

In the postwar years, marketing tapped into the desire to rise through class barriers in what was still a very class-oriented society. The result was a class-focused approach, with product-based marketing stressing the quality of product through the brand.

Through the 1960s, TV advertising emerged as one of the means (perhaps the main means) of marketing communication. Brand imagery dominated brand-marketing theory. Consumer perception of the brand was all-important. The emphasis moved away from the production values of the product. Instead, with the advent of niche marketing in the 1970s, the brand became a door to a particular type of lifestyle. The lifestyle approach focused on consumer differentiation. The brand added value to the physical product. It offered a lifestyle choice through social imitation.

BRANDS ON THE BALANCE SHEET

The 1980s saw the increasing globalization of business take an effect on branding. In an overcrowded product market where reverse engineering and speed to market began to erode the advantages of product differentiation, it became uneconomic to launch a campaign for every brand. Individual brand launches became the province of particularly innovative products. Instead, corporations looked to build a global corporate brand beneath which they could shelter their range of products.

As if the threatened demise of the single-product brand was not enough, an even greater upheaval in the perception of brands was on its way. Against the background of the "greed is good" Gekkoesque late 1980s, many famous brands succumbed to corporate raiders who had realized that the true value of the target company was not its tangible material assets such as machinery or buildings. It was not even necessarily true that the real value in a company lay in its earnings stream. No, the true value of a company lay in its brands, immaterial and intangible though they were. The beauty of it as far as the corporate raider was concerned was that that value of the brand was not reflected in the company's balance sheet.

This was truly a revolution in the understanding of brands. Where once companies had paid seven or eight times earnings for a company, suddenly they were paying 20 to 25 times earnings. Nestlé bought Rowntree Macintosh for three times its market valuation and 26 times its earnings. Inevitably, pressures arose to redress the situation, and soon the accountants arrived at a formula to represent the value of a brand in the bottom line. Interestingly, the formula relied on separating out the brand from other factors that would have necessarily contributed to its real value, such as relationships with other brands and the brand-owning company's reputation – a position that goes against the grain of the contemporary view of brand management as a holistic exercise. The brands landscape had permanently shifted, and brand equity as a tangible asset on the balance sheet had been pushed to the forefront.

THE BRAND BACKLASH

Unfortunately for many of the CEOs at the center of the takeovers and mergers mania, by the time they had sat down and taken stock of the massive corporations and in many cases huge mountains of debt that they had acquired, a brands backlash had begun.

On Friday April 2, 1993, Philip Morris, the US tobacco giant, cut prices of its branded cigarettes, including Marlboro, by a quarter. It was a high-risk strategy, a response to competition from generic, unbranded cigarettes. As it turned out, it was the wrong response – one that called into question the value of brands. Following Marlboro Friday, as it became known, the stock price of Philip Morris, and with it the fortunes of Marlboro, one of the world's leading and legendary brands, fell dramatically, precipitating panic on Wall Street and a crisis of confidence in brands. Analysts took a hard look at the prices paid by companies for brands and questioned whether they had overpaid. Business magazines were quick to sound the death knell for product brands and brand managers. There was no need to ask – the bell tolled for brands.

At the same time, leading management thinkers such as Jerry I. Porras and James C. Collins, Gary Hamel and C.K. Prahalad, and Jean-Noel Kapferer were producing books suggesting that the segregated approach to marketing and brand management was outmoded, outdated and redundant in the new networking age.[2,3] While there were many suggestions as to the future of brands, one consensus was that long-lasting corporate success lay in the ability of a business to harness its intangible assets such as knowledge and culture across internal corporate boundaries, and that this should be a global holistic process. Long-established functional boundaries were out.

A STATE OF FLUX

Today, at the beginning of a new millennium, branding theory and practice are in a state of flux. The power of brands is undeniably strong, at least as far as the leading brands are concerned. Names such as Coca-Cola, Marlboro, Ford, and Microsoft still head the charts of leading brands by valuation.[4]

However, the domination of producer brands has been challenged by own-label distributor brands. In a UK brand survey cited by Kapferer, a list of the top ten brands as symbols of quality included Marks & Spencer, Boots, and Sainsbury – all brands representing distributors.[5] Elsewhere in Europe, the leading Dutch supermarket chain Albert Heijn's own-label products were ranked far ahead of Nestlé's on all criteria – including trustworthiness, product innovation, and packaging as well as price.

The Internet also poses new challenges for those seeking to create and manage brands. On the one hand, the Web has supplemented the marketer's arsenal with a myriad of new techniques to raise awareness of products and brands. It has, however, also denuded some of the mystique of brands. Over the Internet the consumer transaction becomes more transparent. Consumers become increasingly sophisticated, armed with greater product and price information than ever before. To some degree this can strip the risk out of purchasing products – one of the key elements that branding trades on. If it is possible to canvass the opinions of countless other consumers on Websites such as www.epinions.com, the value of the brand as a psychological assurance of quality diminishes.

Worse still is the specter of the "remote shopping bot" visible on the horizon. If and when online shopping really takes off, futurists and technology labs such as MIT Media Labs and Xerox PARC are convinced that e-purchasers of the future will be using a software program or "shopping bot" to carry out transactions on their behalf. When you input the goods you wish to purchase, the bot will venture out onto the Net, compare prices and features, haggle purchases, and arrange for delivery of the chosen goods. And what part will the psychological perception of brands play in this transaction? None.

These are challenging times for marketers as they struggle to come to terms with an increasingly complex consumer market. In this state of flux one thing remains certain, however: brands will continue to evolve and play an essential part in the marketing of corporations and their products and services.

LEARNING POINTS

Evolution of brands:

» as a symbol of ownership – e.g. cattle branding;
» association with reputation – medieval guilds, Vatican court structure;
» recognition of regional/national brands via travelling salesmen in late nineteenth-century US;
» mass market brands – the Model T Ford and the US automobile industry in the 1920s;
» luxury brands – brand differentiation, Sloan and GM;

» brand management – Procter & Gamble, 1931;
» the brand as an assurance of product quality – after World War II;
» lifestyle brands – the 60s and 70s;
» globalization and the rise of the corporate brand – the 80s;
» Marlboro Friday and the brand backlash – the early 90s;
» e-branding.

NOTES

1 Kerry, Kathleen (1996) "GM warms up the branding iron." *Business-Week*, September 23.
2 Collins, James C. & Porras, Jerry I. (1994) *Built to Last: Successful Habits of Visionary Companies*. HarperBusiness, New York.
3 Hamel, Gary, & Prahalad, C.K., *Competing for the Future*. Harvard Business School Press, Cambridge, MA.
4 63.111.41.5/interbrand/test/html/events/table_1.html and www.eterra.com.ar/Informe_Interbrand_2000.htm
5 Kapferer, J.-N. (1997) *Strategic Brand Management*. Kogan Page, London.

The E-Dimension:

E-Branding

Branding on the Internet presents new challenges for e-marketers. This chapter explores the key issues, including:

» the invisibility of the online brand;
» the transparency of markets;
» creating trust online.

"Price does not rule the Web; trust does."
Frederick Reichheld, academic and consultant at Bain &
Company

Despite the trickle of dot-com failures that has threatened to turn into a flood, there can be no doubt that the Internet as a business medium is here to stay. As a new marketing channel the Internet presents a number of challenges for companies who wish to use it as a medium to build or sustain brand equity. For established brands there is first a decision to be made about how to *translate* the brand on to the Net. For Internet pure-plays, the more fundamental question is how to *create* a brand on the Net.

In the case of established brands, some brand theorists believe that it is a mistake to try to make the transition of the brand to the Internet at all. Al Ries, founder of Ries & Ries brand consultants and an acknowledged expert on e-branding, argues that a bricks-and-mortar company trying to become a clicks-and-mortar company is actually diluting the brand. Instead he suggests that a well-known brand intent on setting up business online should do so under a different name. Many companies appear to agree, hence the rash of online banking offshoots with names like Egg (backed by the less hip-sounding Prudential), Smile (the Co-operative Bank) and Cahoot (Abbey National).

Other companies have adopted a halfway-house approach, linking up with an online company to obtain the advantages that the Internet offers without risking the brand. US retailer KB Toys pursued this strategy in a joint venture with the Internet company Brainplay. Drugstore Rite Aid opted for a partnership approach.

Ries suggests some criteria that can be used to determine whether a business is suitable for the Internet. According to Ries, the Internet is particularly appropriate for:

» intangible products such as banking, insurance, and share dealing;
» products sold as commodities rather than as fashionable or luxury goods;
» low-value items;
» products that are available in many different variations – books and CDs, for example;
» businesses where shipping costs are not a factor.

For Internet pure-plays, the decision is not whether to build an online brand, but how. Building brands online is no easy task. For all the millions of dollars spent on marketing, few Internet-only companies have successfully developed strong brands. Yahoo!, Amazon, AOL and eBay are some of the exceptions, and it is surely no accident that these companies are both leaders in their Internet market segments and part of the first wave of dot-coms.

THE INVISIBLE BRAND

There are many reasons why it is difficult to establish a brand on the Net. The French philosopher Descartes once posed a question along the lines of, "How can we be sure the world still exists when we are not directly experiencing it?" Brands on the Internet suffer from the same Cartesian dilemma. Most consumers spend only a small proportion of their lives online. When they are not online, there is no physical evidence of an online brand to remind them of its existence (excluding advertising and PR). BMWs drive past us, Coke cans line the shelves in our supermarkets, bank tellers wearing bank livery hand us money (or we get it from a branded ATM). The real world is, as Tom Peters said, "branded, branded, branded." Everyday life is like one gigantic product-placement exercise; but not for the Internet brands. When the consumer turns off the computer, the brand becomes invisible.

To overcome this aura of invisibility, online brands have to find ways of maintaining a presence in the mind of the consumer when the consumer is offline. This implies big marketing budgets. It has been this need to remain visible that has led to the extraordinary burn rate and consequent downfall of many dot-com companies. Even if its business model is viable, the amount of cash needed for brand building may prove too great a weight around a company's neck. In any case, Ries and other commentators do not believe that the Internet will prove to be a viable medium for the sale of many products other than low-cost commodity products that the consumer does not need to experience before purchasing. Buying a car online may well be cheaper than buying through a car showroom, but how many people are actually going to buy a car over the Internet without wanting to sit in it and drive it?

Brand invisibility is not the only problem facing a company that decides to build a brand on the Internet. There are two other significant challenges to overcome: transparency and trust.

THE NAKED MARKET

Economists at the investment bank Warburg Dillon Read suggest that the new economy should be called the "nude economy", because the Internet makes it more transparent and exposed. The Internet allows buyers and sellers to compare prices. It cuts out the middlemen between firms and customers. It reduces transaction costs. And it reduces barriers to entry.

The implications for businesses are profound. Companies used to be able to present a carefully crafted façade to customers. Brand image was all-important. No matter how poorly organized or cynical things were on the inside, those on the outside could see only what the company wanted them to see. But the Internet is exposing companies as never before to the watchful eyes of consumers.

The business academic Indrajit Sinha has observed that, amid the euphoria surrounding e-commerce, many companies are overlooking a sobering reality: the Internet represents the biggest threat so far to a company's ability to brand its products, charge premium prices and maintain high margins.

Sinha, assistant professor of marketing at Temple University's Fox School of Business and Management in Philadelphia, bases his argument on what economists call cost transparency. An abundance of free, easily accessible information means that consumers can easily compare prices anywhere in the world, and also uncover a wealth of data about product quality, service, and reliability.

"All that information has a way of making a seller's costs more transparent to buyers – in other words, it lets them see through those costs and determine whether they are in line with the prices being charged," Sinha observes. Armed with this information, consumers can put pressure on traditional businesses as well as on those that are trading online.

As a result, companies can no longer hide behind their façades. Thomas Gad, a Swedish branding expert and one of the founders of the Web-branding consultancy Differ, says:

"The New Economy is all about transparency. The Internet has accelerated a process that was already under way. Consumers have greater access to information than ever before. They are able to observe the internal workings of the companies they do business with. As they become more aware of their new power, they will peer into every nook and cranny. Transparent markets demand transparent organizations."

Gad believes that we are on the threshold of a significant change. The route to the transparent market, he argues, has taken business through three distinct stages: product marketing, niche marketing, and the rise of the critical consumer.

According to Gad, we are now entering the next phase: the transparent market. The openness created by the Internet makes this development more dramatic. Production is increasingly controlled by customer values. The result is transparent production, where the customer has full insight, and products that are also transparent, as are the values and knowledge behind them. Everything becomes open to the consumer. Gad says:

"On the Web you are transparent, easily compared with others, in direct contact with your end customer or user or member. You receive an immediate response on every activity. You will be scrutinized. You will be asked questions. There is nowhere to hide.

"In the traditional market, many companies managed to play hide-and-seek and maintain several different roles at the same time for different audiences: sometimes being suppliers, sometimes distributing in their own name, and sometimes being just a know-how partner. Since consumers found it hard to penetrate this, it was never really a problem. In the Web-driven transparent market of today, such a situation is no longer tenable."

In the end, what is left in the nude economy is a simple decision about whether the difference between costs and price – the margin charged by the supplier – represents good value for money. The naked company has nothing up its sleeve. With its brand ruthlessly exposed, it stands or falls on its ability to provide value.

BRAND TRUST

The consulting firm Bain & Company has led the way in exploring the field of customer loyalty. The firm undertook two years of research into e-loyalty. The conclusion of Bain's Frederick Reichheld and Phil Schefter: "Price does not rule the Web; trust does."

"Without the glue of loyalty, even the best-designed e-business model will collapse," they note. This explains why CEOs at the cutting edge of e-commerce – from Michael Dell, to eBay's Meg Whitman – care deeply about customer retention. Loyalty, say Reichheld and Schefter, is an economic necessity. "Acquiring customers on the Internet is enormously expensive, and unless those customers stick around and make lots of repeat purchases over the years, then profits will remain elusive."

In the bright, fashionable, hi-tech world of the new economy, however, the old-fashioned virtue of trust is an elusive quality. A survey of 200 UK Internet users by the advertising agency Leo Burnett found that, despite the millions spent on marketing, consumers still trust traditional company brands more than they trust dot-coms. While name recognition is high, trust is stubbornly low. Lastminute.com was recognized by 84% of people but trusted only by 17%. In contrast, corporations and companies such as the BBC, Boots, and the Prudential have a healthy reservoir of trust to fall back on.

Trust has to be earned – it cannot be created. A salesman who greets new customers with the words "Trust me" is likely to achieve the opposite effect. If trust is predictability and confidence in future behavior, then the new dot-com brands will inevitably struggle to build trust until they have survived long enough to warrant it. Companies such as Coca-Cola, Kellogg, and Ford have built trust over decades. Amazon, Yahoo!, eBay, and others in the dot-com vanguard are only beginning.

Nowhere is the importance of trust better illustrated than in the increasingly fraught world of online banking. The attractions of online banking are obvious. There are cost savings across the board. There is no need for all that bricks and mortar in expensive High Street locations.

There is an opportunity to lighten the payroll load. And online banking brings better, more efficient, instant service whenever customers want it. They can reorder their finances at the dead of night when they are on vacation on a distant beach. The problem is that research suggests that, when it comes to money, consumers prefer bricks to clicks.

In a survey commissioned by the identity consultancy Henrion, Ludlow & Schmidt (HLS), only 7% of people claimed to trust online banks, compared with the 75% who placed more trust in bricks-and-mortar banks.

The findings have far-reaching implications for those responsible for crafting sustainable online brands. As Chris Ludlow of HLS observed: "Trust is essential when building brands, especially in the financial services industry where credibility and security are paramount. Given the new ways of communicating, made possible through advances in technology, it is tempting to believe that brands can now be built overnight. Clearly this is not the case."

Paradoxically, it seems that if, as Al Ries suggests, a bank develops its online brand under a different name – as many banks have – then it is unlikely to benefit from the trust equity associated with its bricks-and-mortar brand.

So, how do you build trust online? The trouble is that, although trust is a simple concept, it is incredibly difficult to build. Says Tony Cram of Ashridge Management College:

"There is more to it than time alone. Counter-intuitively, trust seems to build faster with a series of short interactions, rather than from a single intense experience. DHL, for example, has demonstrated that regularity and frequent touch-points can build trust in a shorter timescale. Similarly, it is no coincidence that the most trusted retailers are those, such as Boots and Tesco, that are visited the most frequently."

The variety of contact with a brand is also important in building relationships. Take Disney, for example. A consumer can experience Disney through Disney movies, by watching the Disney Channel, by shopping in a Disney store, by logging on to the Disney Website, or by visiting Disneyland. A high level of interactivity is associated with these experiences. The greater the perception of a relationship in the minds of consumers, the greater the degree of trust afforded to the brand.

Impersonal transactions between brand and consumer do not have the same trust-building effect and may even denude trust. The increasing depletion of both bank tellers and local branches in the UK has met with considerable consumer resistance and has done the banking brands no good at all. Similarly, a sterile interaction with a Website is unlikely to enhance the trust between the consumer and the dot-com brand. Ironically, in order to build its brand effectively a dot-com may need to provide physical contact, such as by maintaining a High Street presence, or, at least, may need to make excellent customer support permanently available ("excellent" does not describe being held in a telephone queue for over 30 minutes).

One thing in favor of the emergent dot-com brands is that great brands are often forged in adversity. If the dot-coms manage to overcome the pitfalls of the transparent market and build a relationship of trust with their consumers, they will be only part way towards building brands to rival the likes of Coca-Cola. How the dot-com brands of today react to their current problems will, however, have a great bearing on whether they will become the brands of tomorrow.

CASE STUDY: ASK JEEVES

What do you think of when you hear the words, "Ask Jeeves"? The Emeryville, California, company of the same name hopes that the answer is: a jaunty butler holding a tray.

Jeeves, to be found gracing the Website of the natural language search engine at www.ask.com, is one of the best examples of online brand execution that there is. The knowledgeable butler is more than just a presence on the company's Website – although he is on virtually every page. He is more, even, than a mere corporate symbol. A conceptual advance on the average corporate brand, the characteristically dapper Jeeves is the embodiment of the company and its product.

What turned out to be a marketing masterstroke almost never happened. Jeeves nearly failed to pass out of butler school when there were doubts at the company that people would "get" the concept. According to ex-CEO Robert Wrubel, the worry was that people would fail to pick up on the "Ask Jeeves" slogan, mistaking it for "Ask cheese" or even "Ask Jesus".

Luckily, Wrubel and his team trusted their instincts. It was an inspired move. The friendly butler can evoke a wide range of emotions. Deferential yet helpful, personable, friendly, and trustworthy, the butler can be relied on to assist customers by providing the information they need.

Ask Jeeves is not alone in employing a character to represent the brand. There is the Taco Bell chihuahua, the sock from pets.com (now confined to the sock drawer), the ill-fated Miss Boo of boo.com notoriety – and who could forget Ronald McDonald? Ask Jeeves, however, has been careful not to thrust its manservant into the limelight in an unseemly fashion. Instead, he hovers in the background waiting to serve. He was even designed so as not to appear too snobbish, presumably to avoid offending the socialists among us.

Jeeves' heightened sense of discretion did not prevent him from taking part in some pretty high-profile guerrilla marketing campaigns. Academy Awards time saw a bevy of butlers take to the streets serving bottled water from silver trays. In New York's financial heartland, another so-called "butler-blast" saw the butlers pour on to the pavements of Wall Street to hand out copies of the *Wall Street Journal* and *New York Times* in the opening salvo of Ask Jeeves' business campaign.

In keeping with the innovative spirit of many dot-com marketing campaigns, Ask Jeeves has used a variety of channels to get its message across. The company put stickers on 15 million apples, with a question on the sticker next to Jeeves' image asking, "Why is New York called the Big Apple?" The tactic was extended to 60 million oranges, prompting a juicy 30% increase in questions about oranges on the Ask Jeeves Website!

With the amount of interest that Jeeves has provoked in the company that gave birth to him, and with the level of recognition garnered by that paragon of helpfulness, you would be forgiven for assuming that Ask Jeeves is the premier Internet search engine. In fact it is not. The dazzling technology of the search engine beloved of nerds and information-seekers alike, Google, is in many ways superior to that of Ask Jeeves. Yahoo!, one of the few dot-com superstars, is also ahead in the rankings. AltaVista is tough competition. But what these brands lack is personality. No other search engine engenders the loyalty that Ask Jeeves does. It is difficult to imagine an Internet user establishing a relationship with the other search engines or conducting an e-mail dialog addressing the company in person – Jeeves' e-mail inbox is overflowing. This is the value of the brand.

In 2000, Ask Jeeves underwent a corporate restructuring that saw the departure of CEO Wrubel. President and COO Ted Briscoe and Marketing VP David Hellier left for Play Streaming Media Group and over 150 employees had to clear their desks. Despite the upheaval, the company's management was predicting 30% annual growth, and retained over 125 major global corporations as customers. Jeeves, of course, stoically butlers on.

The question of whether the brand is strong enough to maintain the company's position in the top echelon of search engines is a difficult one to answer. Of course, you could ask Jeeves.

Link

www.ask.com

LEARNING POINTS
Should a brand go online? Ries' 5 factors:

» intangible products;
» products as commodities;
» low-value items;
» wide product variety;
» no or low shipping costs.

E-branding – the challenges:

» the invisible brand – brand presence;
» the naked market – market transparency;
» brand trust – e-loyalty.

E-branding – getting it right:

» Ask Jeeves.

The Global Dimension

"One world, one brand" has become a marketing mantra. But is the global brand a good idea? This chapter discusses the challenges of building and sustaining a global brand. These include:

» the rise of the global brand;
» reasons for going global;
» building a global brand;
» case study: McDonald's;
» think local; act local.

"I am irresistible, I say, as I put on my designer fragrance. I am a merchant banker, I say, as I climb out of my BMW; I am a juvenile lout, I say, as I down a glass of extra strong lager. I am handsome, I say, as I don my Levi's jeans."

John Kay, British economist and business commentator

RISE OF THE GLOBAL BRAND

It is not that long since brands were generally, though not exclusively, national in character. Consumer tastes were conveniently assumed to correlate with borders. Thus the British had the steady reliable Morris Minor, Germans had the durable Mercedes, and the French had Citroën's idiosyncratic classic, the *Deux Chevaux*. Today, brands and businesses know no borders. Products are less likely to be predominately German or French in character – they may be European, but are more likely to have no fixed place of birth. Increasingly, brands are cosmopolitan pan-nationals.

One of the triggers for this global attitude towards brands was a theory proposed by one of the leading marketing academics and researchers of the postwar period, Theodore Levitt. In his influential *Harvard Business Review* article, "The Globalization of Markets", Professor Levitt argued that the state of global economic and cultural integration was sufficient to allow the sale of products and services with a consistent marketing and advertising campaign regardless of the country[1] – one brand for many countries.

As a result of Levitt's views on globalization, many corporations were persuaded to reduce their regional subsidiaries' powers of decision-making over their brands. Instead there was a move towards centralization of marketing planning at corporate headquarters.

The rise of globalization was one of the most striking trends in the business world of the 1990s. Brands, to a large extent, led the way. Their flexibility and increasingly international nature mean that it has been automatically assumed in many quarters that particular brands are ripe for a global approach.

Many are. To prove the point, any major international sporting event will feature an array of global brands, whether they are Mars, Coca-Cola, McDonald's, or Hertz. Brands travel well, and global brands have now penetrated virtually every country on earth. Research by Gallup into the brand awareness of the Chinese found that Coke was already the second most popular brand, following Hitachi.

Globalization is a relatively recent phenomenon, fuelled by technology, international travel, and the rise of truly mass media. The emphasis on scalability that most venture capital firms give to dot-com ventures has only served to focus attention on the potential for branding to be applied on a global basis. Some brands, however, recognized the benefits of globalization before it became academically fashionable. Take Hilton Hotels, for example. Conrad Hilton, the group's founder, noticed that hotels were used not just by holiday makers, but by the travelling foot-soldiers of the business world who used them as temporary homes and offices. While hotels crumbled through competition from motels, Hilton invented a lucrative business offering a high-quality, standardized service regardless of where the hotel was located in the world. The global and standardized brand remains firmly in place – the Hilton in Miami is the same as that in Rome or elsewhere. The company even used advertising featuring a taxi in a city with the caption "Take me to the Hilton" – the assumption being that any major city has a Hilton, "where you can be yourself again." Senior managers still flock to Hiltons.

WHY GLOBAL?

For most corporations today, building a global brand is a must. The importance of global brands was summed up by former Unilever chairman Sir Michael Perry:

"The first question to be asked of any successful brand today anywhere is, will it travel? And how fast will it travel? Because you have no time to take this process slowly but surely. If you don't move that successful brand around the world rapidly, you can be sure your competitor will take the idea, lift it and move it ahead of you. Speed to market is of the essence. But the point . . . central to all of this is that a global brand is simply a local brand reproduced many times."[2]

So what are the benefits of globalization? Generally, the benefits cover five key areas of any business:

» *Research and development*. R&D organized on a global basis and aimed toward global markets allows companies to simplify their product range, respond more quickly to market needs, and achieve efficiencies through mutual co-operation.

» *Purchasing*. Global purchasing allows companies to respond quickly to changes in the markets for their raw materials, and to flex their purchasing power more effectively.

» *Production*. Production organized on a global basis can bring economies of scale and cost reductions.

» *Marketing*. In theory, global marketing allows organizations to make more cost-effective use of global media, save costs by eliminating duplication, and share knowledge and experience more easily.

» *Distribution/sales*. With systems geared to servicing a global market, a company's range of products and services should be more readily and more quickly available anywhere in the world

Globalization, it is thought, brings speed, flexibility and cost savings. The company is in tune with and close to all of its markets, no matter where they are located.

The globalization of corporations usually entails some degree of rationalization. Local departments may be subsumed into the corporate headquarters, and there may be significant lay-offs. The approach when globalizing brands is no different. If the costs associated with maintaining one brand are $X and with maintaining ten brands $10X, then it is no surprise that corporations looked to achieve economies of scale by folding the ten brands into one.

BUILDING A GLOBAL BRAND

Once the benefits of a global brand have been accepted, the next questions to ask are: "How does a company go about establishing a brand? And once it has done so, how does it maintain its position?"

Companies must be careful not confuse establishing a global brand with "operating globally". As Robert L. Wehling, global marketing officer for Procter & Gamble, noted:

"Assuming adequate levels of capitalization, anyone can accomplish the former (operating globally); achieving the latter (establishing a global brand) means fashioning a brand that has a clear and consistent equity or identity with consumers across geographies. It is generally positioned the same from one country to another. It has essentially the same product formulation, delivers the same benefits and uses a consistent advertising concept. That isn't to say there isn't room for local tailoring. In fact, there must be room to adapt to local needs."

Focus

It is no easy task building a global brand. There is fierce competition from other corporations seeking to do the same; the marketplace is increasingly crowded with products and services.

Al Ries, chairman of Ries & Ries, the Atlanta-based marketing firm, uses an analogy to illustrate the difference between global and local brand building. "How many stores will you find in a small town?", he asks. The answer is one: a general store that sells everything you might possibly want. In a big city, however, you will find hundreds of specialized stores. This is what Ries calls the global paradox. The larger the market, the more specialized the company and its brands must become. The key is focus. The more global a company, the narrower its focus must become.

Take a uniquely American brand like Chevrolet, suggests Ries. Chevrolet makes a variety of models, cars and trucks, expensive and cheap. Ries argues that in order to become a dominant global brand Chevrolet would have to trade-in many of its existing models for just a few models marketed on a global basis. It's a tough call and one that many corporations are slow or unwilling to make.

Local competition

Then there is the competition from local companies who are in close contact with the market and have the freedom to target their brand.

By its very nature, the globalization of brands raises the possibility of a threat to the hegemony enjoyed by existing leading brands from the developed world. The developed world seems to assume that the globalization of brands equates with the dominance of familiar brands from the developed economies. When brands were operated on a local basis, developing countries faced extreme difficulty in penetrating foreign markets. Now, in an increasingly centralized world, the economies of scale offered by technology and a global approach lower the barriers for a brand's entry to the market.

For the major corporations, however, the penalty for failing to establish a global brand or for mismanaging one can be severe. There are countless upstarts clamoring to knock the leading brands from their perch. Take one eye off the ball and the corporate fumble that follows can be the branding equivalent of a turnover in the dying seconds of the Superbowl. It's not just about corporate pride – it's about the bottom line. Witness Coca-Cola's misconceived response to a perceived threat from the Pepsi taste-test: New Coke could have been irreparably damaged by a brand that, although weaker, might nonetheless have permanently relegated Coca-Cola to #2 position behind Pepsi, had it not been for an astute retrieve by Roberto Goizueta.

Equally, corporate misdemeanors or inappropriate corporate behavior can easily rebound on a global brand and tarnish its reputation. The Barings brand was brought its knees by the trading practices of one of its employees, the infamous rogue trader Nick Leeson. The Japanese banks' brands were tarnished when a series of directors fell on their swords – at one point it seemed almost daily – amidst news stories of financial impropriety. This was not good for brands with personalities centered on (among other qualities) trust.

Implementing an internal culture consistent with the brand's values is only part of the battle for a global brand. It must also struggle to overcome built-in regional prejudices that favor local brands over international ones, a tendency particularly strong in nations such as the UK and the US. Ultimately, global brands aspire to a level of familiarity that leads individuals to consider the brand to be local, regardless of its parenthood.

Global goals

Lippincott and Margulies, the brands consultancy, has identified four essential goals common to corporate global brand strategies:

» *protecting* "core equity elements" – those that are driving market share;
» *fixing* negative equity elements – which represent lost share;
» *attacking* competitors' positive equity elements – neutralizing their brand advantages;
» *leveraging* competitors' negative equity elements – taking full advantage of their weaknesses.

Clearly there are a wide variety of actions that can be taken to attain these goals, depending on how the particular equity element in question is perceived by the consumer.

SUCCESSFUL GLOBAL BRANDS

Despite the tough challenges, hundreds of corporations have made the successful transition to a truly global brand. Absolut, Cisco, Coca-Cola, Microsoft, Nokia, Sony, and Visa are all successful global brands. Each has its own story and its own reasons for success. One feature common to many of them, however, is that they are pioneers in their market segment. Indeed, many were the original, the first to stake a claim in the territory. Dell was the first computer retailer to sell directly online. Coca-Cola sold the first cola. McDonald's was the first fast-food franchise chain.

CASE STUDY: MCDONALD'S

In 1940, when the two McDonald brothers, Dick and Maurice, opened up a restaurant in San Bernardino, California, they could have had no idea that the barbecue and car-hop diner would become the leading global brand of fast-food restaurants.

The key moment in McDonald's rise to fame was probably the day Ray Kroc, a kitchen equipment salesman who sold marketing rights to milkshake mixers, walked across the threshold. By this time the McDonald brothers had moved into fast food, selling hamburgers at a cost of 15 cents, a malt drink for 20 cents, and a pack of fries for 10 cents. Customers could drive in and place their order at the first window. The choice wasn't great, but by the time they'd driven to the next window, their order was ready. The customers loved it.

In 1954 Kroc bought the American franchise to McDonald's for $2.7 mn, and in 1961 bought the world rights. The rest is history. As the McDonald brothers stepped back into branding mythology, Kroc took over the world.

Kroc brought dynamism combined with homespun business philosophy – "Persistence and determination alone are omnipotent"; "If a corporation has two executives who think alike, one is unnecessary"; or try Kroc on helping your neighbor: "If I saw a competitor drowning, I'd put a live fire hose in his mouth." It worked. The hundredth McDonald's store opened in 1959; the first outside the US started in 1967; and, in 1990, the last bastion fell when McDonald's opened up in Moscow. Russians could not buy anything in their supermarkets, but could admire the efficiency of capitalism at work as the entire foreign community in Moscow ate at McDonald's.

The ninth restaurant in the McDonald's chain – and Kroc's first – was in Des Plaines, Illinois. The McDonald's HQ is located nearby at Oak Brook. Today, McDonald's has 28,000 restaurants in 120 countries. In 1999 the company had over 15 billion customer visits.

Branding the world's fast food

The secret of McDonald's global success lies in its focus on its core brands and the ability to translate the McDonald's concept easily across international boundaries. McDonald's has almost half of the globally branded quick-service restaurants outside the US. The formula is astonishingly universal (and international sales account for 60% of McDonald's earnings): limited choice, quick service, and clean restaurants. While McDonald's is successful across the world, there is nothing particularly original or innovative about what it does. You don't have to be one of the Roux brothers to serve up a tasty cheeseburger. Instead, McDonald's does the simple things well. A McDonald's restaurant in Nairobi, Kenya, looks much the same as one in Warsaw, Poland, or Battle Creek,

Michigan. (There are some allowances for local tastes but only where necessary – for instance, lamb burgers in India and kosher burgers in Israel.)

Henry Ford mastered mass product production; McDonald's has mastered mass service production. It has done so through strict adherence to simple beliefs. Quality, cleanliness, and uniformity are the basis of the McDonald's brand. Kroc was an obsessive about these issues. "It requires a certain kind of mind to see beauty in a hamburger bun," he reflected. He was right – no one else manages to do the simple things as well. In effect, the very uniformity of the brand is the crucial differentiating factor. It is, McDonald's proclaims, the "most successful food service organization in the world."

Importantly, despite leading its market, McDonald's is far from complacent. It still possesses the all-conquering self-esteem of a global powerhouse. Its publicity material notes with some regret that "On any day, even as the market leader, McDonald's serves less than one percent of the world's population." There are always more mouths to feed.

THE OPPOSING VIEW

The trend towards global brands is not without opposition. In the more than 15 years since Ted Levitt wrote about the globalization of markets, other academics have voiced their concerns about taking an international, centralized approach to brands. John Quelch, Dean of London Business School, is one such academic. Quelch argues that there are certain advantages to be had in customizing a corporation's approach to branding to suit local markets. No doubt this is a heretical view in the eyes of the "one world, one brand" evangelists.

Quelch cites three points in favor of his proposition.

» The end of the Cold War (and the advance of other developing countries) has created a number of new and emerging markets whose individual cultural and economic needs must be considered in order to develop them as markets.

» Where international corporations have moved into local markets by buying local companies, they confuse the markets by imposing international brands upon the existing local-brand infrastructure.

» Local competitors are increasingly knowledgeable when it comes to marketing techniques. By using their specialist local knowledge, they can make life very difficult for would-be global brands.

Interestingly, global corporations may agree with Quelch's position. Douglas Daft, chairman and CEO of Coca-Cola, was quoted in the *Wall Street Journal* as saying, "Think local, act local." It may be a sign that the global brands have found it more difficult than originally envisaged to penetrate markets beyond the initial segment of willing converts.

When Quelch is speaking on global marketing, he likes to quote from one of John le Carré's spy novels: "You know, a desk is a very dangerous place from which to view the world." And it would seem logical that the longer corporations remain distant from their global markets, the less in touch with those markets they will become. Whether there will be a trend away from centralizing towards localizing remains to be seen. The economies of scale afforded by global brands are often too tempting to be given up easily. The best model may eventually lie somewhere in the middle. The debate will, however, surely continue.

LEARNING POINTS

The global brand advantage:

» R&D
» purchasing
» production
» marketing
» distribution/sales.

Issues around building a global brand:

» focus
» local competition
» global goals.

Global brands - getting it right:

» McDonald's.

NOTES

1 Theodore Levitt (1983) *"The Globalization of Markets."* Harvard Business Review, May-June.
2 *AdWeek*, December 14, 1992.

The State of the Art

Brand theory is constantly evolving. So what are today's hot topics in branding? This chapter explores current trends, including:

» corporate branding;
» branding inside the organization;
» the role of the CEO;
» brand custodianship.

"Companies must be able to describe themselves – both internally and externally – because they are no longer adequately defined by the products they make. Customers buy the company and everything it stands for. So the company must be able to define itself in a connected and coherent way."

Jesper Kunde, Danish branding expert

Branding theory is constantly changing. The last few decades, which included the rise of the hi-tech industries, have seen some of most significant changes yet in the theory of brands. Increasingly, marketing practitioners and academics are questioning the fundamental assumptions of marketing and branding. Does the concept of a Unique Selling Proposition (USP) still hold true? Is it possible to lead in more than one product category with the same brand? Is branding still the responsibility of the marketing department? How far can a brand be stretched? Are brands relevant to hi-tech companies and the Internet? What can be branded and what cannot?

The best way to answer some of these questions and to find out how branding strategy is likely to develop in the new millennium is to take a closer look at what some of the leading thinkers in the field are saying. What are the current trends? What issues are currently up for debate?

THE RISE OF THE CORPORATE BRAND

Corporate branding is one of the most popular marketing trends of the last decade. Many companies such as Virgin have firmly established corporate brands, while others such as Nestlé have flirted with the idea. What are the reasons for this trend – and is it an effective brand strategy?

In a market crowded with products, in a world where consumers are ever more sophisticated, companies are eternally searching for a competitive edge. Quality management, knowledge workers, emotional capital: these are all management straws at which companies have grasped. The corporate brand is yet another concept that appears to offer the promise of competitive advantage.

Ethics

One driver behind the rise of the corporate brand is the growth of pressure groups and the influence of ethical concerns in the corporate decision-making process. Once, factors such as quality, innovation, product range, and price were key brand differentiators – but no longer. In the transparent market they are just the tickets to the game. Instead, companies see areas such as corporate social policy as a means of increasing brand equity – or, in the case of what many consider anti-social practices, damaging it.

A company can use its corporate brand to manipulate the public perception of its image more effectively. And therein lies the attraction of the corporate brand to companies that operate in more controversial markets. Monsanto, a company that markets genetically modified crops, needs to present a human face to the world. In the future, history may well regard companies that are carrying out groundbreaking work in the field of genetics in a favorable light. In the present, however, companies in this field have an image problem – and many see corporate branding as a means of addressing it. The same principle applies to the beleaguered tobacco industry, oil companies, and other companies that have come under similar scrutiny from pressure groups.

For companies not driven by the same need to control the corporate image, there are other factors at play in motivating the adoption of the corporate brand.

Focus

Corporate brands provide focus in an increasingly confusing world. It used to be simple. If you wanted a colored soda, you bought a Coke (or possibly a Pepsi); when you went on a business trip, you stayed in a Hilton Hotel; if you bought some perfume as a gift, it came with the label of a fashion house such as Chanel. Those were the days. Then, suddenly, you could buy a Virgin cola (but isn't that a record label – or is it an airline?), stay in a McDonald's hotel (a burger chain, surely?), or purchase perfume made by Bic (yes, the Biro people).

With this kind of brand extension, it's no wonder consumers are bewildered. Not content with "sticking to the knitting", companies are stretching their brands to breaking point. In a world where everyone sells everything, what is a poor consumer to do? After all, don't consumers rely on companies to tell them which product or service to buy?

The corporate brand provides some clarity among the confusion. A consumer whose attention is focused on the corporate brand has less to choose from and has something different to base that choice on. Instead of deciding which product to buy from the vast array of similar products, consumers decide which company to buy. And they do so because they empathize with, relate to, and trust the brand personality of that company; they know what the corporate brand stands for and they like it.

At least, that's the idea. In reality, however, things are a little more complicated. Launching or building a corporate brand can be an uncertain process. When Kellogg launched its "serving the nation's health" campaign on the back of research from the Henley Centre that suggested Kellogg was the UK's most trusted brand, the company could have expected nothing but success. However, the campaign was short-lived, and Kellogg has now reverted to a more product-led approach.

Concentrating attention on the corporate brand also makes it easier for detractors of a company to target their criticism. Jack Greenberg, the Chairman and CEO of McDonald's, acknowledged that his company "is often the poster child for antiglobalization sentiment." It is a lot harder for critics to attack effectively a company such as Procter & Gamble whose identity remains elusively hidden behind its products than a highly visible company such as Nike or McDonald's.

Another problem with corporate branding is that it is very difficult to measure its effectiveness. When brands were directly related to individual products or product ranges, quantitative analysis was possible, if not easy. When the brand transcends products and product ranges, proving a direct correlation between the brand and the bottom line is tough. In a company culture that is results-driven, management often look for short-term measurements to support their position and shy away from marketing methods where they are unable to point to statistics to justify budgets. (Research by Aaker, Kelly, and Jacobsen into the link between brand equity and stock price may help – see box.) Judging by a survey conducted by Corporate Edge, a division of the international corporate branding and design firm CLK.MPL, companies might be forgiven for having some misgivings about building a corporate brand. Of the leading companies surveyed, 72% said corporate branding was very important to them. Unfortunately for the companies, the consumer was less convinced, with only 45% saying it was very important. Interestingly, fast-moving consumer goods (FMCG) companies also needed some persuasion, with 50% thinking that corporate branding wouldn't rise above product-led branding in importance.

The reasons cited for developing a corporate brand reflected the current debate about the subject. Increased competition (22%) and use as a sustainable strategic tool (21%) were both listed.

Building a corporate brand is not just about corporate image or helping the confused consumer. A corporate brand can provide other benefits for companies, such as giving guidance for employee action and helping to create a clearly defined corporate identity. Regardless of whether the effectiveness of the corporate brand can be measured or not, the benefits may be too important to ignore. Certainly companies seem to think so. In the Corporate Edge survey, 80% of the companies surveyed acknowledged the growing power of corporate branding.

BRANDING TECHNOLOGY COMPANIES

The new economy is dominated by the fortunes of the hi-tech companies. Traditionally these companies have tended to focus marketing efforts on trumpeting their latest innovative products rather than on brand-building exercises. However, the brand valuation of companies such as Microsoft, IBM, and Intel has made many hi-tech companies re-evaluate their marketing strategies.

So is there any hard evidence to support a link between brand equity and improvements in the stock price? David Aaker, Michael Kelly, and Robert Jacobsen think there is. The three academics conducted a study to determine whether there was a correlation between brand-building activities, future profitability, and stock-market returns. Although it was a comparatively limited study looking at quarterly data for the years 1988–97 inclusive for nine companies – Apple, Borland, Compaq, Dell, Hewlett-Packard, IBM, Microsoft, Novell, and Oracle – the results were surprising.

Analysis of the data showed that there was indeed a link between building or damaging brand equity and stock price. For every 1 point increase in brand equity there was a commensurate 1% increase in stock price. This is a substantial effect, given that a 1% increase in earnings is generally held to produce a 1.5% increase in stock price.

If this link holds true for the majority of hi-tech stocks, then it is clear that building brand equity is not merely a cosmetic exercise but is one that directly affects the share price. What hi-tech companies need to know next is: what actions build or have an adverse effect on brand equity? Aaker, Kelly, and Jacobsen identified five factors that influenced attitude towards brands.

Major new products

As a general rule, the introduction of a new product had no discernible effect on brand equity. In this study, however, there were three notable exceptions: IBM's ThinkPad, Apple's Newton, and Microsoft's Windows. All three were supported by massive advertising and publicity campaigns. This was despite the fact that two of the products – the ThinkPad and the Newton – each had a comparatively small effect on total corporate earnings.

Product problems

Consumer disappointment in Apple's Newton, coming as it did after a big buildup for the product, caused a dip in the Apple brand equity. This demonstrates how a sub-brand can adversely affect its parent brand. Another infamous example of product problems damaging brand equity is the Intel floating-point chip defect in 1994. Public perception of Intel in the light of the defect and Intel's initial response to the problem caused the stock price to lose some 11% of its value. Intel's announcement that they would replace all defective chips had the contrasting effect of boosting the stock price by 6%, despite threatening to cost the semiconductor company close on $500 mn to carry out.

In this case, investors clearly valued the long-term sustenance of brand equity over the short-term costs of maintaining that equity.

Change in top management

Senior management maneuverings are perfectly capable of influencing brand equity. This is particularly true in light of the recent trend for CEOs to take a direct interest in a company's brand strategy. In many hi-tech companies, the CEO has come to personify the company itself – its values, its brand. The return of the prodigal son Steve Jobs to Apple and the arrival of Lou Gerstner at IBM in 1993 both resulted in improvements in the company's brand equity.

Competitor actions

Not only can the actions of the company itself affect brand equity, but so can those of its competitors. Hewlett-Packard's brand equity suffered at the hands of a campaign run by Canon extolling the virtues of the bubble-jet technology at the expense of HP products.

Legal actions

Legal actions such as Borland's loss of a major lawsuit over copyright infringement or Microsoft's lengthy battle with the US Government can cause brand equity to fall. Of course, building brand equity is only part of the story. Brand equity has eventually to be translated into earnings and profits. What the study demonstrates, however, is that hi-tech companies can no more afford to ignore brand equity than can traditional companies. Building a strong brand should figure in any hi-tech company's strategic vision. Furthermore, advertising is not enough to maintain brand equity. Companies should pay attention to other factors that influence brand equity, such as those outlined by Aaker, Kelly, and Jacobsen.[1]

BRANDING AND ITS PLACE WITHIN THE ORGANIZATION

If the inevitable rise of the corporate brand is accepted, the next question to ask is: how does the corporation go about building that brand? What kind of relationship should the company have with its brand?

Following in a long line of original thinkers from Scandinavia, Danish branding expert Jesper Kunde has some clear and insightful ideas on the relationship of the brand within the organization. Based in Copenhagen, Kunde worked at Carlsberg and at the electronics company LK before starting his own advertising agency, Kunde & Co., with partner Gaute Hogh in 1988.

In his book *Corporate Religion*, Kunde asserts that branding is not just about the marketing of a company's products and services but is the key to the strategic positioning of the entire business. Indeed, he goes further, claiming that creating and sustaining the brand is the future role of management. Brand power in the ''outside'' market, he says, is a direct by-product of the internal soul and personality of the firm. What a company does/makes/sells is inseparable from what it is. Authenticity is everything. He continues:

> ''Companies must be able to describe themselves – both internally and externally – because they are no longer adequately defined by the products they make. Customers buy the company and everything it stands for. So the company must be able to define itself in a connected and coherent way.''

Despite the provocative title, in *Corporate Religion* Kunde offers not just a new perspective on branding but a radical re-framing of the bond between customer, employer, and employee. He claims that branding in the future will have to go much deeper, embodying the personality and corporate soul of the company. Defining the brand will be the primary task of senior managers.

To be successful, he argues, companies have to create their own brand religion: a religion that brings together the internal company culture and the external market position through a mutual set of beliefs. (The word "religion" derives from the Latin *religare* – to bind something together in a common expression.)

Kunde describes his concept of *Corporate Religion* as:

> "that which expresses the soul of a company and supports the building of a strong market position. In order to make a Corporate Religion come alive you have to describe your internal organization as well as your external market. These internal values create an internal movement that delivers the whole heart and soul of the company."

Furthermore, Kunde believes the world is entering a new era, which he calls the "value economy". If the industrial economy was about the product and the marketing economy was about branding, then the value economy Kunde envisages is about uniqueness.

In the branding economy the focus was on communication of the brand values to the consumer. Companies battled to win the minds of the customer. Today most companies have mastered the art of communication. However, in the value economy, Kunde argues, the brand will be the key management tool in creating something with a unique value that is capable of being communicated globally.

Brand custodianship

If Kunde is right, there are profound implications for management. Leaders of organizations will have to become involved in defining and communicating the corporate brand to the world. Success will not be about the size of the company but about which companies build the strongest brands. In this process the CEO becomes the custodian of the brand.

The Corporate Edge survey suggests that companies already recognize the growing role the CEO has to play in brand strategy: 58% of companies said that the CEO was guardian of the brand, while 42% plumped for the marketing director.

The changing role of the CEO is old news in the US, where the leaders of companies are increasingly on the front line meeting, greeting, and communicating the corporate brand to their customers. Take some of the world's biggest brands: their leaders are famous across the globe – such people as Bill Gates at Microsoft, Steve Jobs at Apple, John Chambers at Cisco, and Michael Eisner at Disney. Elsewhere the process of transformation in the CEO's role is slower, but bosses such as Richard Branson of Virgin and Julian Richer of Richer Sounds are showing the way. All these business leaders understand the importance of the brand as an asset of the company, and they understand the need to communicate the brand personally.

One of the reasons for the success of companies such as Coca-Cola, Microsoft, and Virgin is that brand management is a top-down process. The CEOs recognize the strategic and material value of the brand. They become involved in the "internal branding" process. Instead of the brand wrapping around the business, the business is built around the brand. To align the organization with the brand, to synchronize the values of the workforce with those of the brand, needs sanction from top-level management. If it's CEO-driven, it gets done.

Turnarounds such as those at IBM and Apple show what can be achieved when the CEO backs the brand. Arriving at IBM in 1993, Lou Gerstner has transformed a company that was too product-driven. Pigeonholed as a retailer of PCs and mainframes, IBM was left at the starting gate when the Internet revolution took off. Gerstner understood the value of the IBM brand and focused the company around the brand rather than around any one particular product. The result? IBM is back in business; it leverages its brand to supply a range of products and services backed with the brand's assurance of quality. In 2000 Big Blue ranked #3 in the Interbrand brand rankings with a value of $53,184 bn.

Apple is another example of the difference that it makes to a company if the CEO is in tune with the brand. In the early 1990s Apple got into serious trouble: it shed CEOs in quick succession, lost market share, and for a time looked as if it might disappear altogether. Enter Steve Jobs, stage left. Who better understood the Apple brand than its co-creator? Jobs galvanized the tired company by refocusing on the brand personality. The new iMac product range was just the stroke of genius the market had come to expect from Jobs. More importantly, however, it was just the kind of stylish innovation that the world expected from the Apple brand.

The quality that these brand-aware CEOs share is a desire to suffuse the brand values into the corporation and the workforce. To do this they need to have acute marketing savvy. Most do not come from formal marketing backgrounds. The preferred route to the corporate summit has traditionally been through finance, accountancy, and general management. All brand-aware CEOs, regardless of their backgrounds, realize the benefits of marketing.

Marketing as a separate function within the organization has fallen from favor over the last decade or so. With CEOs championing the brand, the marketing function may stage a revival. The nature of marketing the brand is, however, irrevocably changing as its effective "internal marketing" becomes critical. As marketing gains favor, more marketers are likely to make it to the top of the corporate ladder, increasing the number of brand-aware CEOs.

However, research carried out for the Marketing Society by Taylor Nelson Sofres, marketing information consultants, suggests that the process will be a slow one. Only 16% of UK companies required all their directors to meet the consumer regularly, and a staggering 43% required it of none.

Things are a little better in the customer-service-oriented US. A good example of a CEO in touch with his customers is Herb Kelleher, CEO of Southwest Airlines, repeatedly voted best businessman of the year in the US. Kelleher frequently travels economy on his own airlines to canvass the opinions of passengers. (Maybe it's an airline thing, as both Richard Branson of Virgin Airways and Stelios Haji-Ioannou of EasyJet, both UK companies, conduct similar exercises.)

In their roles as custodians of the brand, CEOs will need to be out among the crowds. The days of the motorized cavalcade are over; pressing the flesh and sounding out opinions in person, both internally from the employees and externally from consumers, is the order of the day. This kind of communication might not come naturally for many CEOs. Like it or not, they will have to learn.

BRANDING THE INDIVIDUAL

Branding is not just for corporations. In the New Economy there has been a gradual erosion of the unspoken contract between companies and employees to provide lifetime employment. Instead there has been a continual move towards freelance contracting and short-term contract employment – the so-called free-agent nation.

In the late 1990s Tom Peters, the management writer, wrote an article in *Fast Company* that urged individuals to adopt the branding strategy of corporations.[2] Like all brilliant ideas, it seemed obvious when Peters explained it.

Companies have spent a great deal of money developing their brand strategies. They have taken into account the advice of academics, researchers, practitioners, and commentators and distilled it into a workable and effective brand strategy. We know it's effective, because there are few people who do not have some sort of relationship with a brand. Whether it's the logo on the trainers, the badge on the car, or the label on the clothes, nearly everyone is branded.

In the free-agent world, argues Peters, we are in effect all CEOs of our own companies. There is therefore no reason why individuals cannot create a buzz about themselves in the same way that Sony does about its PlayStation – albeit with a smaller budget.

The starting point in defining a personal brand is to look for the qualities that differentiate the individual. What differentiates me from others? What are my key personality traits and characteristics, the qualities – call them what you will – that define me as a person?

Companies frequently use a feature-benefit model when they create brands. For each feature offered by a product or service, a corresponding benefit to the consumer should be identifiable. Once individuals have grilled themselves sufficiently, asking questions such as, "What do I do that adds measurable, specialized added-value? What have I done in the past that I can use to enhance my brand equity?", then they should have gained an understanding of their brand values.

The next step is to market the brand. In today's society there are no prizes for shyness or modesty. Peters characteristically recommends that individuals "market the bejesus" out of their brands.

As with corporate brands, maintaining a high level of visibility is crucial for marketing the individual's brand. Networking, "presenteeism", and attending and conducting meetings at work all enhance visibility. It is important to remember, however, that with visibility come potential pitfalls. Some companies, Intel for example, have found out to their cost how easy it is to damage brand equity. Individuals seeking to create their own personal brand have to be constantly vigilant. Behavior must be consistent with brand identity at all times.

And as in most marketing, there is a place for style. Appearance matters when a brand is being judged. After all, branding is about claiming a place in the mind of the consumer. In personal branding, credibility and power are must-have qualities. Some of the most powerful brands are those that confer a certain status by association. Similarly, the strongest personal brands will be those with which others wish to be associated. What this means in practice is that the individual must have something others want. Skills, contact, good company – they all count. Individuals should ask why others would want to associate and be associated with them. It's to be hoped that coming up with an answer won't be too much of a struggle. Whatever the answer is, cultivate it. Once individuals have effectively marketed themselves, they will acquire the Holy Grail of individual branding – a reputation.

Peters' take on branding the individual might seem lighthearted and frivolous. It is anything but. Peters is spot-on in his observations. In the new world of work the successful individuals will be those who have created their own brands. It's already the case. How many times do we hear that a successful person has charisma, personal magnetism, expertise in a particular field, an easygoing charm? Whether by design or not, these people have created their own brands. They have established their reputations. And there is no reason why others who would wish to emulate their success should not consciously create their own brands. The power of brands is not limited to soft drinks and motor cars.

As Peters says: "It's this simple: You are a brand. You are in charge of your brand."

LEARNING POINTS

Contemporary branding issues:

» rise of the corporate brand – ethics, focus;
» brand equity and stock market price – Aaker, Kelly, Jacobsen survey;
» branding in the organization – Jesper Kunde and corporate religion;
» whose brand is it anyway? – the CEO as brand custodian;
» Personal branding – Tom Peters and Brand U.

NOTES

1 Aaker, David A., Kelly, Michael Kelly, Jacobson, Robert. "Brand News". *Business 2.0* Website at www.business2.co.za/infront/ebusiness/124240.htm

2 Peters, Tom (1997) "The Brand Called You." *Fast Company*, August 10.

In Practice: Branding Success Stories

What are the secrets of creating a great brand? This chapter explains how Intel, Toyota, Virgin, and Coca-Cola have managed to create some of the greatest brands of all time. It includes case studies of:

» Intel's "Intel inside" strategy;
» Coca-Cola;
» Virgin;
» Toyota.

"Well-managed brands live on, only bad brand managers die."
George Bull, British executive and brand champion

INTEL

In 1968, Gordon Moore and Robert Noyce left Fairchild Semiconductor to establish their own company, Intel. The rest is a whirlwind of technological history and huge commercial success. The two original founders were joined in their adventure by employee #4, Andy Grove; and, along the way, Gordon Moore came up with Silicon Valley's most quoted law. Moore's Law states that the number of electronic elements that can be written on the same-sized chip will double every 18 months.

The technological leaps forward started early in Intel's life. In 1971 it introduced the world's first microprocessor, the 4004. Intel also invented the high-speed memory (DRAM) used in every kind of computer system. Such was its success that Intel had 10,000 employees by 1977. In the 1980s, it shrewdly refused to give other manufacturers a license to make its most powerful chips – so it made them all. In 1981, IBM launched its PC, based on the Intel microprocessor. This helped sales reach $1 bn for the first time in 1984. A blip in 1986 saw Intel record a loss for the first time, but it speedily returned to profit in 1987, and in 1990 racked up its first $1 bn quarter, followed three years later by its first $2 bn quarter.

Branding the component

For most of this time, Intel was unbranded and unknown. Only Silicon Valley insiders and computer enthusiasts are really interested in where the chips come from. Even though it already held over 80% of the PC-chip market, Intel decided that it wanted to become a known brand as well as hugely successful. Intel wanted everyone to be aware what was doing the real work inside computers. The result was its "Intel Inside" campaign, which was hugely expensive and successful. People are now aware that Intel makes chips. From nowhere, Intel became a top-ranking brand. By 1993 Intel was voted the world's third most valuable brand by *Financial World* magazine. Valued at $17.8 bn (its nearest competitor was worth $4.1 bn), Intel lagged behind only Marlboro and Coca-Cola. Quite an achievement.

Intel followed up its initial campaign with one for its Pentium chip. The logic behind this was that the Pentium was the newest and most powerful PC chip on the market. The Pentium was Intel's successor to the highly successful 266, 386, and 486 chips.

After its launch at the beginning of 1994, Intel anticipated that sales of the Pentium would reach over 10 million units by 1996. The campaign encouraged people to switch from 486 machines to Pentium PCs. It worked, increasing awareness of the Pentium. In fact, it worked so well that it left companies such as Compaq needing to find a way of persuading the public that the 486 was not obsolete.

Of course, having revealed to the world that it makes the chips, Intel's troubles begin if the chips go wrong. It may be three million transistors on a minute bit of silicon, but we expect it to be perfect and, thanks to Intel's marketing, if there is a fault in the chip we now know who to blame. Forget Dell or IBM – call Intel.

When the chips are down

"With Intel Inside you know you've got ... unparalleled quality," read an Intel advertisement. The "unparalleled quality" boast appeared a little excessive late in 1994 when Thomas Nicely, a mathematics professor at Lynchburg College, Virginia, achieved international renown. Professor Nicely found that his three Pentium computers were making mistakes. In an effort to get to the bottom of the mystery, he shared his discovery on the Internet. Thanks to the miracles of modern technology, a minor mathematical problem became an international incident. And, thanks to Intel's advertising, people knew where the fault lay.

In December 1994, IBM announced that it was halting shipments of the affected PCs and Intel was forced to adopt a vigorous damage-limitation exercise. Intel's first reaction was that IBM's tests were "contrived".

Whatever the nature and regularity of the flaw, Intel clearly had set itself up. Ironically, the problem with the Pentium was far less significant than flaws found in previous chips – the only difference was that Intel had marketed the brand too successfully. Not only had five million Pentiums been manufactured, but the Pentium was also backed by an $80 mn marketing campaign to encourage the market to make the switch from the old (the 486) to the new (the Pentium). This came on top of the estimated $70 mn spent on the Intel Inside campaigns.

Intel's problems were largely of its own making. It created the brand and had to live with the consequences. Also, it was clearly a victim of its own success. The bigger the name, the bigger the brand, and the keener that competitors, onlookers, commentators, and journalists are to topple it from its pedestal.

After a hesitant start Intel eventually, in December 1994, offered to replace processors free of charge. "Our previous policy was to talk with users to determine whether their needs required replacement of the processor. There was resentment to our approach – it appeared that we at Intel were arrogant, we were telling customers what was good for them. Maybe we have been thick-headed ... but we finally figured it out," observed Andy Grove.[1] On December 22, Intel took out full-page advertisements to apologize:

> "No microprocessor is ever perfect. What Intel continues to believe is that an extremely minor technical problem has taken on a life of its own. Although Intel firmly stands behind the quality of the current version of the Pentium processor, we recognize that many users have concerns. We want to resolve these concerns."

As Moore's Law predicts, such distractions quickly become history. Technology and Intel move on. The focus of Intel's marketing has moved from selling product features in the early 1970s to direct partnership with the final customers of the company's microprocessors. It has moved on with remorseless speed and a rare clarity of purpose and thinking.

BRAND INSIGHTS: INTEL

» Intel's masterful marketing of the Pentium microprocessor was one of the first and finest instances of a company successfully branding a component. Despite the Intel chip being invisible to the end user, the company still managed to convince people that it was essential to have an "Intel Inside". It's a great example of the power of branding in the right hands.

» Once a company has established a brand, it has a responsibility to its customers. As Sir Michael Perry, the former Unilever chairman, puts it: "You buy the brand because you consider it a friend. That trust, that sense of reliability and confidence is the reason you invest in it. The whole definition of a brand is about that kind of predictability and security ... But if you betray that trust, then the consumers are going to be quite long in forgiving."[2] Intel almost lost the trust of its consumers during the saga of the defective Pentium chips. Fortunately, after a slow start the company promised to replace the processors in question, thereby salvaging the brand equity before it was irretrievably damaged.

INTEL SNAPSHOTS

» 1968 – Company founded by Gordon Moore and Robert Noyce.
» 1971 – Intel introduces the world's first microprocessor, the 4004.
» 1984 – Sales reach $1 bn.
» 1993 – Intel voted #3 most valuable brand in the world by *Financial World*.
» 1994 – Pentium flaw comes to light; Intel offers to replace processor free of charge.
» 2000 – Intel ranked #4 in Interbrand's survey of the world's most valuable brands.

TOYOTA

In 1918, Sakichi Toyoda formed a company called the Toyoda Spinning & Weaving Co. In the 1930s the development of automatic looms convinced the company that its future lay elsewhere. Kiichiro Toyoda, the founder's son, had studied engineering and visited the US and Europe. He decided the future lay in car making and changed the company's name to Toyota in 1936. (The name "Toyota" emerged from a competition – the Japanese characters convey speed and use eight strokes, a number suggesting prosperity. From the Western perspective it is pronounceable and attractively meaningless.) Kiichiro Toyoda remained as company president until 1950 and the company was run by a member of the Toyoda family until 1995.

The first Toyota car was the Model AA. (As something of an insurance policy, the company also continued in its old business – looms were still produced until the early 1950s.) In the 1950s Toyota established offices in Taiwan and Saudi Arabia. It began making forklift trucks (and is now the world's number one in that market) and entered the market in the US (1958) and later in the UK (1965).

Its initial foray into the US proved unsuccessful. Its Crown model was designed for the Japanese market and was ill suited to American freeways. Eventually Toyota got it right. In 1968 the success of the Corolla enabled it to make a great leap forward – by 1975 it had replaced Volkswagen as the number one importer of automobiles into the US. It got right into the heart of the American market in 1984 when it entered into a joint venture with General Motors to build Toyotas in the US. (The joint venture also makes the GM Prizm.)

More successes have followed. The Camry was the best-selling car in the US in 1997. Toyota is now developing its interests in "hybrid-electric" cars – launched in Japan in 1997. It is also involved in financial services, telecommunications and housing, marine engines and recreational boats, parts distribution, and aviation services.

Lean production

Toyota is now the third biggest car maker in the world, behind GM and Ford. In Japan it is the dominant car manufacturer. It now sells approaching 1.5 million cars in the US every year.

Central to this huge success is the simple fact that, in terms of production, Toyota has constantly remained a step ahead of its Western competitors. The reason for this can be seen if you go into Toyota's headquarters building. There you will find three portraits. One is of the company's founder; another is of the company's current president; and the final one is a portrait of the American quality guru, W. Edwards Deming. While Western companies produced gas-guzzling cars with costly, large, and unhappy workforces in the 1970s, Toyota was forging ahead with the implementation of Deming's ideas. In the early 1980s, Western companies finally woke up and began to implement Deming's quality gospel. By then it was too late; Toyota had moved on. (In fact, it didn't mind telling Western companies all about total quality management for this very reason.)

Toyota progressed to what became labeled "lean production", or the Toyota Production System. (The architect of this is usually acknowledged to be Taichi Ohno, who wrote a short book on the Toyota approach and later became a consultant.) From Toyota's point of view, there was nothing revolutionary in lean production. In fact, it was an integral part of the company's commitment to quality and its roots can be traced back to the 1950s. It was only in 1984, when Toyota opened up its joint venture with General Motors in California, that the West began to wake up and the word began to spread.

The word was based on three simple principles. The first was that of just-in-time production. There is no point in producing cars, or anything else, in blind anticipation that someone will buy them. Waste (*muda*) is bad. Production has to be closely tied to the market's requirements. Secondly, responsibility for quality rests with everyone, and any quality defect needs to be rectified as soon as it is identified. The third, more elusive, concept was the "value stream". Instead of the company being viewed as a series of unrelated products and processes, it should be seen as a continuous and uniform whole, a stream that includes suppliers as well as customers.

Luxury Lexus

Toyota's production philosophy and the carefully developed strength of its brand reached its high point in 1990 with the launch of the Lexus. The Lexus was initially greeted as a triumph for Japanese imitation. Media pundits laughed at the company's effrontery – "If Toyota could have slapped a Mercedes star on the front of the Lexus, it would have fooled most of the people most of the time."

Where the Lexus really stole a march on its rivals was through the Lexus ownership experience. Even when things went wrong, the service was good. An early problem led to a product recall. Lexus had dealers call up people personally and immediately. Instead of having a negative effect, it strengthened the channel. Lexus screwed things up like everyone else, but then they sorted the problem out in a friendly, human way. With the Lexus, Toyota proved that its capacity to stay ahead of the pack remains undiminished.

BRAND INSIGHT: TOYOTA

When Toyota wanted to move into the luxury car market, it faced competition from a range of established brands, including stalwarts of the market segment such as Mercedes and BMW. Undaunted by the size of the task, Toyota created a new brand, the Lexus, to create psychological distance from Toyota's other value-for-money car models.

Then, in a masterstroke of brand strategy, it neutralized any concerns over the reliability and quality of the product by out-engineering Mercedes and BMW. Toyota is keen to tell you that the Lexus took seven years, $2 bn, 1400 engineers, 2300 technicians, and 450 prototypes, and generated 200 patents. Its standard fittings include a satellite navigation system and much more. Toyota made great play of the fact that the car was tested in Japan on mile after mile of carefully built highways that exactly imitated roads in the US, Germany, or the UK. Toyota even put in the right road signs.

Add in the excellent ownership experience and it becomes apparent how Toyota was able to pull off what seemed an impossible task and take on the might of the German marques in what were previously considered impregnable markets.

TOYOTA SNAPSHOTS

» 1918 – Sakichi Toyoda forms the Toyoda Spinning & Weaving Co.
» 1936 – The company focuses on car automobile production; renamed Toyota.
» 1958 – Toyota enters the US market (UK in 1965).
» 1968 – Toyota Corolla is a breakthrough car in the US.

> » 1975 – VW replaced by Toyota as #1 importer of autos into the US.
> » 1990 – Toyota muscles into the luxury car market with the Lexus.

VIRGIN

"I believe there is almost no limit to what a brand can do, but only if used properly," says Richard Branson, founder of the Virgin empire. In the past two decades, Richard Branson has re-written the rules of branding.

Branson's greatest achievement to date is to create what is arguably the world's first universal brand. Other famous names have become synonymous with the product they adorn: Hoover vacuum cleaners, Coca-Cola, and Levi Strauss, to name just a few. But Virgin is alone among Western brands in its ability to transcend products. Never before has a single brand been so successfully deployed across such a diverse range of goods and services. It has been used to sell everything from condoms to financial services, bridal gowns to the Sex Pistols.

The most important aspect of the Virgin brand proposition is its credibility among its market segment. Just as existing Virgin products and services provide credibility for new offerings, the relationship between Virgin family members could also work in reverse. If the image were to become tarnished by association with a shoddy product, poor service, or an offering that was a rip-off, then the standing of the wider Virgin brand could be damaged.

Yet despite its remarkable success, Branson would have us believe that none of it was planned. He gives the impression that the Virgin phenomenon is one of those odd things that happen to people sometimes. This is part of the Branson mystique. He makes it look and sound so simple.

"When we came up with the name 'Virgin' instead of 'Slipped Disc' Records for our record company in the winter of 1969, I had some vague idea of the name being catchy and applying to lots of other products for young people.

"It would have been interesting to have tracked the success of the Virgin companies or otherwise if we had called the company Slipped Disc Records. Slipped Disc Condoms might not have worked as well."[3]

The quip is typical of a man who has lived his whole life as if it was some big adventure. An outspoken critic of business schools and management theory, Branson likes to portray himself as the ordinary man on the street (despite his comfortable middle-class origins). He is the small guy who outsmarts the big guys. His account of how the famous Virgin logo came to be is typical of the way things seem to happen at Virgin.

"When Virgin Records became successful we followed our instincts. Initially the music reflected the 'hippy' era and our logo of a naked lady back to back reflected that too. Then when Punk came along we felt we needed a crisper image ... Rather than spending a fortune coming up with the new image, I was talking to our graphic designer one day explaining what we wanted and he threw on the floor his doodling – the now famous Virgin signature – which I fortunately picked up on the way to the loo."

It sounds so casual, but the words mask an extraordinary entrepreneurial mind, one that has re-invented business to fit the times he lives in. Today, Branson is the driving force at the center of a web of over 200 companies, employing more than 25,000 people with global revenues of over £3 bn. His commercial interests span travel, hotels, consumer goods, computer games, music, and airlines. You can even buy a Virgin pension or investment plan.

Financial services are a far cry from the adolescent record label that helped put punk on the map in the 1980s, with a controversially named album by the Sex Pistols. By then, Virgin had already won the respect of the hippy generation with *Tubular Bells*, from a young unknown artist called Mike Oldfield. *Never Mind the Bollocks* was the perfect product to establish the Virgin brand with a new generation of spiky-haired teenagers. Branson had created a new fusion of rebellion and business – and discovered a unique new brand proposition. He has been repeating the formula ever since.

As Branson has matured, so too has the Virgin appeal, originally aimed at younger people. Branson says:

> "Four years ago we crossed over into appealing to their parents. Now we're moving into pensions and life insurance. We haven't quite reached funeral parlors. But we have to be careful we don't lose the kids. I'd like people to feel most of their needs in life can be filled by Virgin. The absolutely critical thing is we must never let them down."[4]

By the mid-1990s, the Virgin name seemed to be everywhere. So ubiquitous had the Virgin brand become that hardly a day seemed to go by without seeing a grinning Richard Branson launching some new Virgin product or service. The famous flying V logo was emblazoned on aircraft, megastores, and movie-theater fronts, and was about to make its debut on cola cans.

The activity prompted some to question whether the Virgin brand was being diluted. Those who understood what he was about, however, recognized that what Branson had created was an entirely new kind of brand proposition. John Murphy, chairman of the famous brand consultancy Interbrand, for example, observed that:

> "Unless they poison someone or start applying the brand to inappropriate products such as pension funds or photocopiers, I doubt whether the Virgin brand will ever be diluted."

Little did Murphy know that by 1996 Virgin Direct would be offering financial services – including pensions.

Branson has acknowledged time and time again that the most vital asset Virgin has is the reputation of its brand. Put the Virgin name on any product that doesn't come up to scratch and the whole company is brought into disrepute. "Our customers trust us," he says simply.

The Branson philosophy, then, is: look after your brand and it will last. There is, however, and always has been a tension at the heart of the Virgin brand. For all his unquestioned emphasis on the integrity of the Virgin name, one of Branson's personal characteristics – one that has become a strand of what Virgin stands for – is a certain restlessness.

He has an insatiable desire to take risks and to explore new areas. It is in his blood that Branson has to be constantly expanding the borders of the empire. Yet it is vital to do so without damaging the good name of the company. This creates something of a dilemma. It is one of which Branson is well aware:

> "We are expanding and growing our use of the brand, but are always mindful of the fact that we should only put it on products and services that fit – or will fit – our very exacting criteria."

In recent years, he has thought long and hard about what the Virgin brand stands for. He believes the reputation the company has built up is based on five key factors: value for money, quality, reliability, innovation, and an indefinable, but nonetheless palpable, sense of fun. (Another, slightly snappier, version of the Virgin brand values is: genuine and fun, contemporary and different, the consumers' champion, and first class at business-class price.[5])

In a classic piece of reverse engineering, these are now the brand values that Virgin applies when considering new business ventures. Branson says that any new product or service must provide, or have the prospect of providing:

» the best quality;
» innovation;
» good value for money;
» a challenge to existing alternatives;
» a sense of fun or cheekiness.

Virgin claims that nine out ten projects it considers are potentially very profitable, but they are rejected if they don't fit with the Group's values.[6] However, Branson says: "If an idea satisfies at least four of these five criteria, we'll usually take a serious look at it."

BRAND INSIGHT: VIRGIN

One of the most frequently asked questions about Virgin is how far the brand can stretch. Some commentators believe that by putting the Virgin name on such a wide range of products and services, Branson risks seriously diluting the brand. His answer to this criticism is that as long as the brand's integrity is not compromised, then the brand is infinitely elastic.

Surveys repeatedly show just how powerful the Virgin brand is. A recent survey found that 96% of British consumers have heard of Virgin and 96% can correctly name Richard Branson as its founder. One commentator notes:

> "Virgin is a unique phenomenon on the British business scene. It has, essentially, one principal asset, and an intangible one at that – its name. From financial services through airlines and railways to entertainment, megastores and soft drinks, clothes and even bridal salons, the brand is instantly recognizable to the consumer, conjuring up an image of good quality, cheap prices, and a trendy hipness that few others can match."[7]

Recently the Virgin brand has suffered some setbacks. Virgin Trains received some well-publicized criticism over its performance. Further, Virgin cried off in its cola war with Coke and Pepsi by withdrawing Virgin cola in February 2000. The company also, surprisingly, failed to win the UK National Lottery franchise when it was open to bids. Yet despite these difficulties, Virgin's brand seems to be undiminished in strength – a testament to the brand equity its unconventional leader has accumulated.

VIRGIN SNAPSHOTS

» 1969 – Richard Branson chooses "Virgin Records" over "Slipped Disc Records" as a name for his new venture.
» 1977 – Branson signs The Sex Pistols to the Virgin record label.
» 1983 – Virgin brands cover some 50 companies.
» 1984 – Virgin Atlantic commences flights to the US.
» 1992 – Virgin Music Group sold to Thorn EMI.

» 1996 – Virgin brand extended to financial services via Virgin Direct.

» 1999 – The Virgin empire numbers over 130 companies.

COCA-COLA

No text about branding would be complete without taking a closer look at the global brand phenomenon that is Coca-Cola.

In May 1886 in Atlanta, Georgia, a pharmacist called Dr John Styth Pemberton came up with a brain tonic. John Pemberton's brain tonic contained a leaf from a South American tree, and West African seeds as well as caramel, phosphoric acid, and a combination of seven "natural flavors" – a formula that remains a well-protected secret to this day. Pemberton's bookkeeper, Frank Robinson, named it Coca-Cola. In a moment of inspiration Robinson also wrote the name with a slanting flourish.

Pemberton's drink was first sold at a soda fountain in Jacob's Pharmacy in Atlanta by Willis Venable. It sold for 5 cents a glass. During its first year on sale, sales averaged six a day.

Today, more than 900 million Coca-Colas are sold every single day. Every second, 12,000 people buy one of Coca-Cola's brands. Coca-Cola is the best known global brand. Currently it is available in virtually every country in the world – the exceptions are countries such as Libya and Iran where its absence is a matter of politics rather than of taste.

Putting the fizz into Coke

It is easy to assume that Coke became a global brand effortlessly in less sophisticated times. In fact there are good reasons for its global success.

The company backed the brand from the very start. John Pemberton spent $73.96 on banners and advertising coupons during his first year, despite revenues of only some 50 dollars. Coca-Cola realized the power of mass media long before many other companies that had been established, much longer. According to the records, Coca-Cola's first ad appeared a mere three weeks after Pemberton invented the drink. It ran in *The Atlanta Journal* and proclaimed:

"Coca-Cola. Delicious! Refreshing! Exhilarating! Invigorating! The New Pop Soda Fountain Drink, containing the properties of the wonderful Coca plant and the famous Cola nuts."

Later, Coke advertisements – proclaiming it to be "delicious and re-freshing" – were featured in Georgia school reports.

Shortly before he died in 1888, Pemberton and his son sold the rights to Coca-Cola to Asa Candler (1851–1929). Candler – later Mayor of Atlanta – was also an advertising enthusiast (and, among other things, a doctor, pharmacist, property developer, and entrepreneur). Among his initiatives was the distribution of thousands of vouchers giving free glasses of the drink. "Soft drink, hard sell" has been the central dichotomy of Coca-Cola's existence.

Cleverly, Coca-Cola's sales pitch was all-American. Early ads featured baseball star Ty Cobb, and other ads provided idyllic views of American life. In 1931 Coke took this further by recruiting Father Christmas as an enthusiastic drinker (some attribute our modern image of Santa as a jolly white-bearded, ruddy-cheeked man dressed in red to Coca-Cola's advertising).

While Coke's advertising attracted customers, the packaging of the product also changed. Progress brought the curvaceous Coke bottle, one of the great images of the twentieth century. It was the result of a design competition held in 1915 and won by the Root Glass Company (the competition, of course, was a smart marketing ploy). In a memo to senior managers, the company's legal counsel said: "We need a bottle which a person will recognize as a Coca-Cola bottle even when he feels it in the dark." The bottle differentiated the brand and added to the brand's identity. (Coca-Cola only became available in cans in 1955.)

Candler's children eventually sold the company to another Atlanta businessman, Ernest Woodruff, for the then massive sum of $25 mn. In 1923, Ernest's son Robert Woodruff (1890–1985) became company president. During Woodruff's long tenure – surely one of the longest in corporate history – Coke continued to develop people's awareness of the product. Its Coke Bathing Girls calendars were a fixture in American drugstores during the 1930s. It looked further afield early on in its life. Indeed, it later looked to the skies – returning Apollo astronauts were welcomed with a sign reading, "Welcome back to earth, home of Coca-Cola."

Back on planet Earth, a foreign sales department was set up as early as 1926. Internationally, its reputation was cemented during the Second World War when it boldly and ambitiously promised that any US soldier would be able to buy a Coke for a nickel. The Coke became the symbol of American taste and consumption. To fulfill its promise, Coca-Cola built 60 mobile bottling plants and sent them along with the army. Each could be run by two men and produce 1370 bottles an hour.

The war cemented Coke's place at the heart of American society. *Time* magazine celebrated Coke's "peaceful near-conquest of the world." The postwar years saw Coke expand its corporate empire in the quest for what it engagingly called "share of throat." New drinks were added to its range. These included Fanta, Sprite, and TAB. None hit the heights of the original brand.

In the 1970s, doubt entered the Coca-Cola empire for the first time. Pepsi-Cola upped the pressure with the Pepsi Challenge. Coke had to open its eyes to the possibility that it had real competition. After a remarkable reign, Woodruff gave way to Roberto Goizueta (1931–97) in 1981.

New Coke, new problems

In most ways, Goizueta's rule was a huge success. When he died in 1997, the company was valued at $145 bn, compared with $4 bn when he had taken over the top job. Surprisingly, Goizueta led Coke into the acquisition of Columbia Pictures in 1982. Though a nightmare to manage, this turned out to be a smart deal. Just a few years later, Coca-Cola sold Columbia to Sony, making a profit of nearly $1 bn. Goizueta also oversaw the successful launch of Diet Coke.

Unfortunately, Goizueta also presided over one of the great marketing gaffes of all time. In 1985 Coca-Cola announced to the world that it was replacing its traditional-recipe cola with New Coke. In detailed research it had discovered that most consumers preferred the new recipe. It was, they said, smoother, sweeter, and preferable to the old version. It was a major strategic mistake. For a start, the old version was selling in many millions every day of the week. The move made the invincible Coca-Cola brand look weak in the perception of consumers by reacting to the threat of its rival Pepsi instead of shrugging off the threat in the manner of the market leader that it was. Further, by producing a drink named "New Coke", the company decoupled its brand values of tradition and authenticity from its new product. To call this the marketing own-goal of the century would be to understate the effect only slightly. Coke was faced with a barrage of criticism.

Fortunately, the management didn't let pride and stubbornness get in the way of good marketing. Realizing that its move had been disastrous, Coke backtracked and, after 90 days, re-introduced the original Coke. It has not been tinkered with since. Overall, however, Goizueta's leadership re-invigorated the Coke brand. Ill in hospital, Goizueta commented: "It's all right if people want to worry about me. But they shouldn't worry about the company, because it's in better shape than it's ever been."

BRAND INSIGHT: COCA-COLA

When Coca-Cola announced an extension of the brand to a range of clothing, since rolled into Europe, the company was at pains to emphasize that the clothing would reflect the Coca-Cola brand values of authenticity, genuineness, and being part of people's lives. It had learnt the lesson of how important the brand values of the company are when it severed the tie between those values and its product New Coke, and suffered as a result.

The difficulty for Coca-Cola is that it is restricted by the phenomenal success of its main product. On the one hand, the brand values mean that possibly the best brand development strategy is to leave well alone. It's difficult to innovate and update the brand while maintaining the traditional feel. The problem associated with this is that it is difficult to take the brand elsewhere. Consequently, unlike for Virgin, brand extension has always been difficult for Coca-Cola. Commentators believe this may prove a significant challenge for Coca-Cola in an era when many global corporations are stretching their brands to squeeze the last drop of equity from them.

COCA-COLA SNAPSHOTS

» 1886 – Dr John Styth Pemberton develops a brain tonic using a secret formula. His bookkeeper Frank Robinson names it Coca-Cola.
» 1888 – Rights sold to Asa Candler.
» 1915 – A design competition produces the classic twisted-glass Coke bottle.
» 1931 – Coca-Cola recruits Father Christmas to its advertising campaign.
» 1926 – The company sets up a foreign sales department.
» 1985 – CEO Roberto Goizueta presides over introduction of New Coke.
» 90 days later – original Coca-Cola brought back.
» 2000 – Coca-Cola #1 in Interbrand's survey of the world's most valuable brands.

NOTES

1 Kehoe, Louise (1994) "Intel offers to replace Pentium microchips." *Financial Times*, December 21.
2 www.marketing.haynet.com/feature00/0330/.
3 Branson, Richard (1998) Lecture shown on *The Money Programme*. BBC.
4 Rodgers, Paul (1997) "The Branson phenomenon." *Enterprise Magazine*, March/April.
5 Campbell, Andrew & Sadtler, David (1998) "Corporate breakups." *Strategy & Business*, 3rd quarter.
6 Virgin Group literature.
7 See note 4.

Key Concepts and Thinkers

Branding has its own language. Get to grips with the lexicon of brands through the *Express Exec* branding glossary in this chapter, which also covers:

» key concepts;
» key thinkers.

"Branding is all about timing. When a company loses time, it creates space for other companies – or new entrants – to take the lead. Companies forget that branding is, sometimes, like a Formula One race. The issue is not being in the race or completing it; it is about finishing in positions 1 or 2."

Jean-Noël Kapferer, French academic and branding expert

Like many other subjects, the theory and practice of branding has a language of its own. What follows is a glossary containing a few of the more common terms associated with branding, as well as a more in-depth look at some of the key concepts and thinkers.

A GLOSSARY OF BRANDING

Brand – A proper noun attached to an individual, firm, product or service. (For a more complete definition, see Chapter 2.)

Brand architecture – The corporate structure delineating relationships between different parts of the brand. It explicitly defines the relationship between the masterbrand, sub-brands, and products/services.

Brand audit – An in-depth examination of all aspects of a particular brand.

Brand building – Increasing a brand's equity.

Brand equity – See Key concepts below.

Brand extension – The extension of a brand to products and services not normally associated with the core brand. Producing sub-variants of an existing branded product is **line extension**. Applying a brand to an entirely different product is brand extension. The Virgin brand is the most commonly cited example of how to extend a brand successfully.

Brand identity – See Key concepts below.

Brand image – The mental perception of the brand in the minds of consumers. This is developed through communications and experience of the brand, and includes the distinguishing "human" characteristics of brand personality (e.g. warm, friendly, fun, or strong). The concept of brand image is also closely aligned with that of brand positioning – although positioning tends to suggest action on the part of the company in assigning attributes to the brand, as opposed to brand image, which is more about consumer perception.

Brand manager – The person in the organization who is responsible for the management of a particular brand.

Brand promise – The explicit or implicit covenant between the company and the consumer to continue to deliver the specific benefits and qualities attributed to a brand.

Brand strategy – The long-term strategic plan for the use of the brand within the marketing strategy of a firm. It includes such things as target market, for example.

Brand values – See Key concepts below.

Corporate identity – The visible elements (name, logos, symbols, signs, packaging, etc.) that can be used to identify a company, as well as the invisible attributes perceived through a company's actions and through personal experience that make up the ''personality'' of the organization.

Image attributes – Attributes important in defining the personality and style of a brand, to help differentiate one brand from competing brands or from similar products and services.

Image criteria – A shopping list of the desired attributes of a company, product, or service that make up its ''personality''.

Logotype (Logo) – A specific and unique group of letterforms or symbols that signify the firm brand – protected by trademark.

Masterbrand – The dominant brand of the organization, which may shelter sub-brands within it.

Message – The information that is most relevant to the target audiences and that serves as a reference for all communications connected with the brand.

Naming – The strategic and creative discipline of choosing the most suitable word(s) to identify an organization, product, or service. The process includes the creation of a list of candidate names – **name generation**.

Naming hierarchy – A means of associating practice groups, subsidiaries, sub-brands, products, etc. with the parent firm.

Positioning statement – A reference statement reflecting the brand's value proposition. It will usually cover three areas: who we are and what we do (**definition**); the benefit to the consumer (**deliverables**); and how we do it differently (**differentiation**).

Sub-brand – A brand beneath the masterbrand in the brand hierarchy.

Symbol – A non-typographic element used to form part of a brand's identity – Apple Computing is a good example, as are many of the automobile marques.

KEY CONCEPTS

Brand equity

Whilst there is no one authoritative and universally accepted definition of brand equity, there are a number of characteristics common to some of the more generally accepted definitions that are offered.

The parties with an interest in brand equity are many, including the corporation, the marketing channel, and the financial markets. Probably the most important of all, however, when it comes to defining brand equity is the consumer.

Some leading researchers in the field of brands have offered the following comments about brand equity:

> "... a set of brand assets and liabilities linked to a brand, its name and symbol, that add to or subtract from the value provided by a product or service to a firm and/or that firm's customers."
>
> *David A. Aaker (1991)[1]*

> "... brand equity represents the value (to a consumer) of a product, above that which would result for an otherwise identical product without the brand's name. In other words, brand equity represents the degree to which a brand's name alone contributes value to the offering (again, from the perspective of the consumer)."
>
> *Lance Leuthesser* et al. *(1995)[2]*

> "The set of associations and behaviors on the part of the brand's customers, channel members, and parent corporations that permit the brand to earn greater volume or greater margins than it could without the brand name and that gives the brand a strong, sustainable, and differentiated advantage over competitors."
>
> *The Marketing Science Institute (1988)*

In his book *Building Strong Brands*, David A. Aaker suggests that an analysis of brand equity (for the purposes of including its value in the accounts) should cover the following areas: price premium, satisfaction/loyalty, perceived quality, leadership/popularity, perceived value, brand personality, organizational associations, brand awareness, market share, market price, and distribution coverage.

From the definitions available it is possible to identify three distinct components of brand equity:

» the notion of the financial value of a brand as a distinct asset capable of representation on a company's balance sheet – we can think of this as *brand valuation*;
» the degree of attachment of the consumer to the brand, or *brand loyalty*;
» the description of the associations and beliefs that a consumer has about a brand – which may be called *brand description*.

These three concepts intertwine to constitute brand equity.

Brand identity

Brand identity is a concept that has recently been brought to the forefront of brand theory. A good explanation of the key components that comprise a brand's identity comes from Jean-Noël Kapferer, a leading exponent of the concept. Kapferer uses the model of a six-sided prism to represent brand identity. The six facets of the prism are:

» **Physique**: This represents a combination of independent characteristics, which may be either manifest or latent.
» **Personality**: A brand acquires a personality through communication about the brand, and experience of the brand and those people identified with the brand.
» **Culture**: The brand has its own culture, which the product physically embodies. Culture implies a system of assumptions based on underlying values.
» **Relationship**: A brand is a relationship. The consumer may have a relationship with the brand. The brand may provide a conduit for

an intangible relationship with other people through association and commonality.

» **Reflection**: A brand reflects a customer's image. It provides a common point of reference for the customer and others. For example, BMW drivers may identify themselves with the brand, and in turn be identified by it. Kapferer says that there is often confusion between this reflection and a brand's **target**. The latter, however, describes the brand's potential purchasers or users.

» **Self-image**: Kapferer claims that through our attitude towards certain brands we develop a type of inner relationship with ourselves. (BMW drivers may come to see the brand as an extension of themselves.)

Brand positioning

There are many factors associated with the positioning of a brand in the marketplace. Of these the three that are most essential for creating a clear brand definition are vision, meaning and relevance.

Vision: the brand's direction

In branding terms, the vision relates to a company's *raison d'être* and signifies where the company is heading, assuming in this instance that there is a single corporate brand capable of identification. The vision need not necessarily be a lofty ideal, although in some commentators' opinion a vision should ideally be unattainable, thus providing a driving force for the company. There are many corporations, however, that express their vision in simple terms – for instance, Merck's "to preserve and improve human life", an example of an aspirational but sustainable vision.

Meaning: the brand in the mind of the consumer

Before marketers can attempt to position the brand in the marketplace, they need to determine exactly what the brand stands for. The brand's meaning is then expressed through the creation of image attributes. Future decisions made about a brand will use the brand's image as a touchstone. Some might argue that marketers can never position the brand in the marketplace; all they can actually do is to send out signals about the brand, and the positioning is all done by the consumer's psychological perception.

Relevance: the brand's core

Brands, to varying degrees, are usually capable of extension. The secret is to understand the brand boundaries – the limits beyond which a brand fails to be true to itself. Stretching a brand too far may not only result in failure of the particular brand extension but may damage the core brand.

Relationship: the brand and its peer group

A brand's positioning must always be considered in the context of its competitors. Brands do not live in isolation. Consumers' perceptions of a brand are colored by the brand choice in the market segment.

Brand values

Brand values are the essence of the brand, often expressed in key words such as quality, creativity, luxury, and integrity. Tom Blackett of Interbrand has suggested that brand values can be divided into three classes:

» *functional*: what the brand "does" for the consumer;
» *expressive*: what the brand "says" about the consumer;
» *central*: what the brand and the consumer "share" at a fundamental level.

Co-branding

Co-branding is where two or possibly more independent brands, often from different corporations, join forces to support a new product or service. This practice is becoming increasingly popular so as to squeeze the last drop of competitive advantage from a brand.

The practice enables brands to increase their sphere of influence, enhance their reputation by association, deliver economies of scale, and make use of new technologies more efficiently.

Co-branding often takes place where the economics of the market do not justify the launch of a new brand or formal joint venture. All brands involved will retain their individual brand names, and usually the brands will be roughly equal in terms of public recognition.[3]

KEY THINKERS

David A. Aaker

David A. Aaker is Professor Emeritus at the Haas School of Business at the University of California, Berkeley. He is also vice-chairman of the brand consultants Prophet Brand Strategy. An alumnus of MIT and Stanford University, Aaker is an acknowledged world authority on brand equity and brand strategy. He has published over 90 articles and 11 books, including *Managing Brand Equity: Capitalizing on the Value of a Brand Name, Developing Business Strategies*, and *Building Strong Brands*. His most recent book is *Brand Leadership* (co-authored with Erich Joachimsthaler), which explores the issue of strategic brand leadership and its implications for the organization.

Aaker lists his research interests as brand strategy, visual imagery, and metaphors.

As a result of his groundbreaking work, Aaker has won a number of awards, including best article published in the *California Management Review* and the *Journal of Marketing* as well as the 1996 Paul D. Converse Award for outstanding contributions to the development of the science of marketing.

At least two of his books, *Building Strong Brands* and *Managing Brand Equity*, are essential reading for anyone with a serious interest in the theory and practice of brands.

In *Building Strong Brands*, Aaker demonstrates, using case studies such as Saturn, General Electric, Kodak, McDonald's, and Harley-Davidson, how to create a strong brand identity; develop brand equity; and organize for brand building. Aaker says of brands:

> "A company's brand is the primary source of its competitive advantage and a valuable strategic asset. Yet, too often, the brand message to customers is weak, confused, irrelevant, or, worst of all, indistinguishable from competitor offerings. The challenge for

all brands is that they have a distinct, clear image that matters to customers and truly differentiates them from the rest.''

Aaker suggests that one key step towards effective differentiation is to create a broad brand vision or identity that elevates a brand to something more than a set of attributes susceptible to copying.

In *Managing Brand Equity*, the book that cemented Aaker's place as a leading commentator on brands, he demonstrates the value of a brand as a strategic asset and a company's primary source of competitive advantage. Aaker explains the concept of brand equity and how it must be implemented. He defines the relationship between the brand and its symbol and slogan. He also examines real-life cases to demonstrate the benefits of brand equity and the pitfalls that await those who seek to create it. The Ivory soap story, the troubles of Schlitz beer, and the manufacture of the Ford Taurus are all featured in the book along with many others.

Link

www.haas.berkeley.edu/~market/PROFILES/PROFS/aaker.html

Highlights

Books:

» (1995) *Building Strong Brands*. The Free Press, New York, NY.
» (1991) *Managing Brand Equity*. The Free Press, New York, NY.
» (1998) *Developing Business Strategies*, 5th edn, John Wiley & Sons, New York, NY.
» (1998) *Strategic Market Management*, 5th edn, John Wiley & Sons, New York, NY.
» (2000) *Brand Leadership*. The Free Press, New York, NY.

Articles:

» (1997) ''Should you take your brand to where the action is?'' *Harvard Business Review*, **75**:5, 135–43.

» (1997) (with Eric Joachimsthaler) "Building brands without mass media." *Harvard Business Review*, **75**:1, 39–50.
» (1994) (with Robert Jacobson) "The financial information content of perceived quality." *Journal of Marketing Research*, **31**:2, 191–201.
» (1994) "The Saturn story: building a brand." *California Management Review*, **36**:2, 114–33.

Jean-Noël Kapferer

Jean-Noël Kapferer has been described as the "classy epitome of conceptual elan." A professor at the HEC School of Management in Paris, Kapferer has injected new life into the debate about brand strategy. With a postgraduate degree in economics from the Sorbonne and a PhD in marketing from Northwestern University, one of the world's premier business schools for marketing, Kapferer is one of the leading marketing thinkers in the world.

His book *Strategic Brand Management*, first published in 1992 and subsequently revised and reprinted in 1996, is an essential read. In this thought-provoking and groundbreaking book, Kapferer proposes three branding models: the Prism, the Pyramid, and the Platform. These are models for three different types of brand: the Prism is for single brands; the Pyramid, for multi-product brands; and the Platform, for rejuvenating brands.

Although the book concentrates on Kapferer's theories about brand management, he also takes the time to examine what exactly constitutes a brand, takes a look at the culture of branding, and provides a cohesive overarching philosophy for all aspects of brand management. The book has hundreds of real-world examples that Kapferer uses to support his case.

One of the world's greatest marketing experts, Philip Kotler, said of *Strategic Brand Management*: "The art of building sales is, to a large extent, the art of building brands. After reading Kapferer's book, you'll never again think of a brand as just a name. Several exciting new ideas and perspectives on brand building are offered that have been absent from our literature."

Further insights into Kapferer's theories on branding are revealed by the branding axioms he holds to be true. They include such pithy aphorisms as: "Brands are nothing more than what their managers do with them"; "The concept of identity is central to managing brands over time"; and "Brand identity is not something you shop for or borrow from someone."

Highlights

Books:

» (1997) *Strategic Brand Management: Creating and Sustaining Brand Equity Long Term*. Kogan Page, London.
» (2000) *Strategic Brand Management: New Approaches to Creating and Evaluating Brand Equity*. DIANE, New York, NY.

Philip Kotler

Philip Kotler is the S.C. Johnson & Son Distinguished Professor of International Marketing at Kellogg Graduate School of Management, Northwestern University.

While leading the marketing debate over 30 years, Philip Kotler has coined phrases such as "mega-marketing", "demarketing", and "social marketing". His numerous books include the definitive textbook on the subject. Kotler has a penchant for useful definitions:

> "When I am asked to define marketing in the briefest possible way, I say marketing is meeting needs profitably. A lot of us meet needs – but businesses are set up to do it profitably. Marketing is the homework that you do to hit the mark that satisfies those needs exactly."

Kotler also provides a useful definition of a product as "anything that can be offered to a market for attention, acquisition, use, or consumption that might satisfy a want or need." He says that a product has five levels:

» the core benefit ("Marketers must see themselves as benefit providers");
» the generic product;
» the expected product (the normal expectations that the customer has of the product);

» the augmented product (the additional services or benefits added to the product);
» the potential product ("all of the augmentations and transformations that this product might ultimately undergo in the future").

Kotler regards marketing as the essence of business and more:

"Good companies will meet needs; great companies will create markets. Market leadership is gained by envisioning new products, services, lifestyles, and ways to raise living standards. There is a vast difference between companies that offer me-too products and those that create new product and service values not even imagined by the marketplace. Ultimately, marketing at its best is about value creation and raising the world's living standards."

Link
www.kellogg.nwu.edu/faculty/bio/Kotler.htm

Highlights
Books:

» (1999) *Marketing Management*, Millennium (10th) edn. Prentice Hall, Englewood Cliffs, NJ.
» (1999) *Kotler on Marketing: How to Create, Win and Dominate Markets*. The Free Press, New York, NY.

Ted Levitt

The American academic Ted (Theodore) Levitt re-ignited serious study of marketing in the early 1960s. Later he was the first to explore some of the marketing implications of globalization. Levitt is the Edward W. Carter Professor of Business Administration Emeritus at the Harvard Business School and former editor of the *Harvard Business Review*.

The July–August 1960 issue of the *Harvard Business Review*, launched Levitt to international fame. It included his article entitled "Marketing myopia", which brought marketing back on to the corporate agenda.

In the article Levitt argued that the central preoccupation of corporations should be with satisfying customers rather than with simply producing goods. Companies should be marketing-led rather than production-led and the lead must come from the chief executive and senior management. "Management must think of itself not as producing products but as providing customer-creating value satisfactions," he observed.

Levitt's other major insight concerned the emergence of globalization. As he had done with "Marketing myopia", Levitt signaled the emergence of a major movement and then withdrew to watch it ignite:

"The world is becoming a common marketplace in which people – no matter where they live – desire the same products and lifestyles. Global companies must forget the idiosyncratic differences between countries and cultures and instead concentrate on satisfying universal drives."

Highlights

Books:

» (1962) *Innovation in Marketing*. McGraw Hill, New York, NY.
» (1969) *The Marketing Mode*. McGraw Hill, New York, NY.
» (1983) *The Marketing Imagination*. The Free Press, New York, NY.
» (1991) *Thinking About Management*. The Free Press, New York, NY.

Levitt's *Harvard Business Review* articles include:

» "Advertising: 'The Poetry of Becoming.'" (March 1, 1993)
» "The case of the migrating markets." (July 1, 1990)
» "After the sale is over." (September 1, 1983)
» "The globalization of markets." (May 1, 1983)
» "Marketing intangible products and product intangibles." (May 1, 1981)
» "Marketing success through differentiation – of anything." (January 1, 1980)
» "The industrialization of service." (September 1, 1976)
» "Marketing myopia." (September 1, 1975)

» "Production-line approach to service." (September 1, 1972)
» "Why business always loses." (March 1, 1968)
» "Exploit the product life cycle." (November 1, 1965)
» "Innovative imitation." (September 1, 1965)

John Quelch

John Quelch is the former dean of London Business School. The ex-professor of marketing at Harvard Business School is an authority on international marketing and marketing ethics.

Quelch has lectured in over 35 countries and advised numerous Fortune 500 companies, including American Airlines, Apple Computer, Coca-Cola, Colgate-Palmolive, Gillette, General Electric, IBM, and Procter & Gamble. He has written more than 10 books on a variety of subjects from sales promotion to brand auditing, as well as over 50 articles on marketing management and public policy issues in leading journals such as the *Harvard Business Review*, *McKinsey Quarterly*, and *Sloan Management Review*.

Quelch is an acknowledged expert in his field, particularly in the areas of developing international markets. His research interests include brands (brand names), strategy (international marketing), new product development strategy, marketing research (consumer satisfaction), and organizations (business ethics and corporate governance).

As well demonstrating his considerable academic prowess, Quelch is no stranger to the real world of commerce: he was one of the founding directors of Reebok and is a non-executive director of several companies, including WPP, the major international marketing group.

Highlights

Books:

» (1999) (with C. Bartlett) *Global Marketing Management*, 4th edn. Addison Wesley, Reading, MA.
» (1995) *Cases in Product Management*. Irwin, Homewood, IL.
» (1994) (with P. Farris) *Cases in Advertising and Promotion Management*, 4th edn. Irwin, Homewood, IL
» (1992) (with R. Buzzell and E. Salama) *The Marketing Challenge of Europe*, 2nd edn. Addison Wesley, Reading, MA.

» (1989) *How to Market to Consumers*. John Wiley & Sons, New York, NY.

» (1989) *Sales Promotion Management*. Prentice-Hall International, London.

Al Ries

Al Ries is a well-known brands strategist, pioneer of the concept of "positioning", author of *Focus*, co-author of the best-selling book *The 22 Immutable Laws of Marketing*, and a branding consultant of over 40 years' experience.

Together with his daughter Laura, Ries has written a book that takes a wry and incisive look at how some of America's top corporations have handled their brands. The authors lay down the laws that in their opinion "make the difference between success and failure in the marketplace" for a company's brand. They answer a range of commonly asked questions such as "Is advertising more important than PR?", "Should a brand go global?", and "How often should a slogan be changed?".

With rules such as The Law of Publicity, The Law of Consistency and The Law of Extensions. Al Ries and his daughter lay down a best-practice code of conduct for companies seeking to use their brand effectively in today's marketplace.

Highlights

Book:

» (1998) (with L. Reis) *The 22 Immutable Laws of Branding: How to Build a Product or Service into a World-Class Brand*. HarperBusiness, New York, NY.

NOTES

1 Aaker, David A. (1991) *Managing Brand Equity*. Free Press, New York, NY.

2 Leuthesser, L., Kohli, C.S. & Harich, K.R. (1995) "Brand equity: the halo effect measure." *European Journal of Marketing*, **29**:4.

3 A good resource is: (1999) Blackett, T. & Boad, R. (eds) *Co-Branding: The Science of Alliance*. Macmillan Press, London.

Resources

Countless words have been written about the subject of branding. This chapter identifies the best branding resources:

» Websites;
» books and articles on branding.

''We are the CEOs of our own companies: Me Inc. To be in business today, our most important job is to be head marketer for the brand called You.''

Tom Peters, business commentator

ADAGE.COM/ADAGEGLOBAL.COM

Established in 1995, AdAge.com is one of the leading Websites for marketing, advertising, and media news. According to many studies, it is the leading industry portal in its market, with over a million page views per month and over 150,000 pages of searchable archives free to the user.

The already popular Website is planning a major relaunch in 2001, adding features such as 29 special reports throughout the year, exclusive online editorial features, and customizable e-mail alerts.

Interconnected with the AdAge Website is its other online offering, AdAgeGlobal.com. Like AdAge.com, it runs a print version in tandem with its online entity.

Ad Age Global is one of the few publications – possibly the only one – to provide such an authoritative and in-depth analysis of the world's advertising, marketing, and media industries.

The print and online versions between them offer a range of features including: commentary on the key industry issues across the globe; a chance to see the latest and best new commercials from around the world; feature interviews with key industry figures; and access to AdAge Global's online statistical database.

The quality and extent of the content on adAge.com and adAgeglobal.com make them must-see destinations for all marketers.

Links

www.AdAge.com
www.AdAgeGlobal.com

ADVERTISING RESEARCH FOUNDATION AND THE *JOURNAL OF ADVERTISING RESEARCH*

The *Journal of Advertising Research* is published bimonthly. Produced by the Advertising Research Foundation, it is sent to individuals in member companies as a part of their membership package. It is also possible, however, to subscribe to the online version.

Its publisher, the Advertising Research Foundation (ARF), is a nonprofit, corporate-membership association and one of the leading professional organizations in the field of advertising, marketing, and media research. Its membership includes over 400 advertisers, advertising agencies, research firms, media companies, educational institutions, and international organizations.

The ARF conducts a great deal of primary research in its field. In the 1990s, for example, the ARF's key research achievements represented an investment of over $4 mn.

The *Journal of Advertising Research* covers a variety of subjects of interest to marketers. For example, the June 2000 (Volume 40, No. 3) Advertising Creativity edition carried an article "Customer/brand loyalty in an interactive marketplace" by Don E. Schultz and Scott Bailey as well as a section on Internet-specific issues.

Link

www.arfsite.org

THE AMERICAN MARKETING ASSOCIATION

The American Marketing Association (AMA) has over 45,000 members in 92 countries, making it one of the largest and most comprehensive societies of marketers in the world. In North America alone there are 500 chapters of the AMA.

Through its professional and collegiate chapters, the AMA provides a means for members to continue their professional education and enhance their career development. The chapters sponsor seminars and workshops and invite leading thinkers from both academia and business to pass on their insights to members. Chapter meetings also provide an excellent means of meeting fellow marketing professionals. There are also a number of national conferences located throughout America.

The AMA publishes a number of magazines and journals that are useful resources for marketing professionals. These include the biweekly magazine *Marketing News* as well as the quarterly magazines *Marketing Management*, *Marketing Research*, and *Marketing Health Services*.

The AMA's four leading-edge journals are *Journal of Marketing*, *Journal of Marketing Research*, *Journal of International Marketing*, and *Journal of Public Policy & Marketing*.

In addition to its magazines and journals, the AMA publishes books tackling the latest topics in marketing and provides a reference center with more than 5000 books, 3000 indexed articles, and 100 periodicals on marketing issues.

Link

www.ama.org

BRANDWEEK

Brandweek magazine and its online equivalent, brandweek.com, are aimed at marketers of the SuperBrands, the top 2000 brands in the US – and at anyone else who takes an interest in some of the most valuable brands in the world.

Part of the same stable as *Adweek* and *Mediaweek*, *Brandweek* provides information on "marketer/retailer relationships, successful media strategies, agency/client relationships, and global marketing." All this plus news, consumer trends, campaigns, promotions news, and details of the latest new brands.

On the Website some features are referred to as premium services and require subscription. However, many features are free to the user, such as the opportunity to peruse news and feature articles.

To give you an idea of the information available on the brandweek.com Website: a typical midweek edition carried stories on Reebok and Leo Burnett as well as a feature on brand extension and Kraft Philadelphia cheese.

It is easy to navigate from the site to adweek.com and mediaweek.com. Together the three make a suite of Websites that all marketers should bookmark.

Links

www.brandweek.com
www.adweek.com
www.mediaweek.com

EMARKETER.COM

Building the brand online is often a dot-com's biggest spend. Before you start signing checks, a little information won't go amiss. Marketing advice and statistics are available on the Internet from a variety of sources; but to save all that browsing time, pay a visit to eMarketer.com.

eMarketer is recognized as an authority on online marketing. The Website provides a comprehensive resource for anyone interested in e-commerce. Information from hundreds of leading research sources is aggregated, filtered, organized, analyzed, and put up on the Website in easy-to-understand tables, charts, and graphs.

There are 11 channels, including B2B e-commerce, B2C e-commerce, e-demographics, e-advertising, broadband, and wireless. Sections include e-reports, in-depth analysis of specific market segments, e-news, and up-to-date news and analysis on industry issues.

One especially useful area is the statistics section. Here surfers can get the lowdown on e-commerce spending figures, demographic trends on the Internet, and other information essential for planning an online marketing campaign, or assessing the market when writing a business plan.

An e-newsletter is available. E-mailed to over 30,000 market professionals every week, it encapsulates the main points from the Website. It is free, but visitors need to register before they can receive it.

Link

www.eMarketer.com

THE INTERBRAND GROUP

The Interbrand Group is one of the world's leading branding consultants. It covers the range of brand-related services commensurate with a consultancy of its size and reputation. These include brand strategy, corporate identity, name development, package and product design, brand research, brand valuation, and trademark law.

The company was founded in London in 1974 to provide specialized services connected with brands and branding. Over the years Interbrand has expanded, opening offices in the United States and Japan. In the 1980s the company pioneered a number of techniques and processes in the field of branding, notably in the areas of brand equity and brand valuation.

In 1993 Interbrand became part of one of the world's leading and largest advertising and communications corporations – the Omnicom Group. Since then Interbrand has ensured that it stays at the forefront of developments in branding by making strategic investments in companies such as Gerstman+Meyers (a top US packaging consultancy), and Newell and Sorrell (a leading corporate identity and design firm).

The Interbrand Group is probably best known for its groundbreaking work in the field of brand valuation. One of the main reasons for visiting the Interbrand Website, apart from checking out information on the range of services it supplies, is to see the ranking for the "World's Most Valuable Brands". You will find the full list of brands ranked by value – Coca-Cola headed the 2000 list.

Link

www.interbrand.com

MEDIA METRIX

E-commerce ventures can spend a fortune on online branding, so how do you make sure you spend your money wisely? How do you check out what the competition is doing? And where do media agencies find out about the state of the industry? The answer to all these questions is: by signing up with one of the companies that track Internet information.

Media Metrix is a leader and pioneer in the field of Internet and digital measurement. The company provides a range of up-to-the-minute audience ratings, e-commerce advertising, and technology measurement services. It has over 750 clients, including leading advertisers, new and traditional media agencies, e-commerce marketers, technology companies, and financial institutions. Clients are offered comprehensive coverage of all digital media, by means of patented metering techniques that measure actual Internet usage behavior in real time, click by click.

Clients can also receive information on what Web marketers and competitors are doing with their online advertising, through the AdRelevance 2.0 advertising measurement service. Its advanced Web-sampling technology is used to measure more than half-a-million URLs, covering over 6000 online advertisements per week.

In September 2000 Media Metrix merged with Jupiter Communications to form Jupiter Media Metrix (www.jmm.com). Reflecting full quarterly results for both Jupiter and Media Metrix, the combined company announced pro forma revenues for the third quarter of 2000 of $38.6 mn, a 113% increase compared to $18.2 mn for the same period in 1999.

Media Metrix charges its clients for the services it provides. Visitors to its site, however, will find some free information – for example, a monthly listing of the sites with the most visitors, both general and categorized by type of business.

Link

www.mediametrix.com

TOTAL RESEARCH CORPORATION

Total Research Corporation is a specialist market research firm with offices across the globe. Although its market research ranges across a variety of disciplines, the firm is particularly well known for its EquiTrend brands surveys.

The annual EquiTrend survey looks at consumer brand perception. It captures the brand preferences of a range of demographic and psychographic segments. The information produced allows marketers to assess their brands' performance in different segments to assess whether their brands are reaching their target markets. The survey asks people to score brands on a scale of 0–10. Total Research's historical benchmarks have shown what these scores really mean: 8.00 is World Class, 7.00 is Strong, 6.00 is Mediocre, 5.00 is Survival Level.

More recently, EquiTrend have launched the EquiTrend Online survey to measure brand equity using Internet technology to obtain in-depth feedback from 30,000 Internet users on their perceptions of the quality of more than 1300 brands in 35 industry categories.

Details of EquiTrend survey findings can be found in the press releases posted on the Total Research Website.

Link

www.totalres.com

OTHER READING MATERIAL

Aaker, David A. and Biel, Alexander L. (eds) (1993) *Brand Equity & Advertising*. Lawrence Erlbaum Associates, Hillsdale, NJ.

Aaker, David A. (2000) *Brand Leadership*. The Free Press, New York.

Arnold, David (1992) *The Handbook of Brand Management*. Addison-Wesley, Reading, MA & Century Business, London.

Bullmore, Jeremy (1998) *Behind the Scenes in Advertising*. Admap, Henley-on-Thames, UK.

Cowley, Don (ed.) (1991) *Understanding Brands*. Kogan Page, London.

Franzen, Giep (1994) *Advertising Effectiveness*. NTC Publications Ltd, Henley-on-Thames, UK.

Howard, Steven (1998) *Corporate Image Management: A Marketing Discipline for the 21st Century*. Butterworth-Heinemann Asia, Singapore.

Kochan, Nicholas (1997) *The World's Greatest Brands*. New York University Press, NY.

MacRae, Chris (1996) *The Brand Chartering Handbook*. Economist Intelligence Unit/Addison-Wesley, Harlow, UK.

Pettis, Chuck (1995) *TechnoBrands*. AMACOM, New York.

Ries, Al & Trout, Jack (1986) *Positioning: The Battle for Your Mind*. Warner Books, New York.

Swasy, Alecia (1993) *Soap Opera*. Times Books, New York.

Trout, Jack with Rivkin, Steve (1996) *The New Positioning*. McGraw-Hill, New York.

Upshaw, Lynn (1995) *Building Brand Identity*. John Wiley & Sons, New York.

Ten Steps to Making Branding Work

Brand theory is one thing; putting it into practice another. This final chapter provides some key insights into creating and sustaining a brand in today's business environment, covering the following steps:

» own minds, not products;
» dare to be different;
» fall in love ("brandlove");
» put a price on the brand;
» make your brand a corporate touchstone;
» know your place;
» get continuous feedback;
» find brand partners;
» protect your brand;
» nurture the brand.

"Any damn fool can put on a deal, but it takes genius, faith, and perseverance to create a brand."

David Ogilvy, advertising executive and thinker

Most texts on branding contain a "ten steps to creating a great brand" checklist. *Branding* is no exception. However, anyone who truly understands the nature of brands will realize that there is no one way of creating a great brand, a brand that will:

» occupy a space in the subconscious minds of millions of people across the world;
» create fierce loyalty from consumers;
» be first on the tips of people's tongues when they are asked to recall a brand in a particular market;
» be instantly recognizable anywhere;
» have a strong brand personality and be true to that personality.

Of course, branding isn't just for the McDonald's, Coca-Colas, and Microsofts of this world. Any company can and should have a brand, whether it is a month old or 100 years old, whether it's a one-person company or has a cast of thousands. All businesses are capable of asking these questions to define their brand: What kind of business is it? What benefits does it confer on its customers? How is it different from the competition? These are the first steps that all companies take on the way to creating their brands.

There is, of course, much more to creating an effective brand than just defining it. While there is no one simple recipe for that perfect brand, there are many ingredients that brands will need, and ideas that brand managers must embrace in order to succeed in the twenty-first century. I am indebted to Thomas Gad for the following ten steps, which draw on Gad's groundbreaking ideas in his book *4D Branding*.[1]

1. OWN MINDS, NOT PRODUCTS

Branding is traditionally centered on a product or service. Coke cans, cars, bank tellers are all physical manifestations of a brand that we see in our everyday lives. Increasingly, however, brands are becoming detached from products or services. They now compete for mind space. The Internet, for example, has introduced a virtual world where it becomes essential to brand the channel. Dissociated from a physical tangible product or service, tomorrow's great brands will have to stake their claim in the minds of the consumer more than ever. Psychological perception is now paramount. So don't think in terms of branding your current products and services; rather focus on planting your brand in the minds of customers. The battle is to capture and maintain a place in their imaginations.

2. DARE TO BE DIFFERENT

Once products strove for uniformity. In the postwar period, mass-market techniques churned out millions of identical products – and that was the selling point. The uniformity of product translated to uniformity of quality in the mind of the consumer. Today, mass markets are fragmenting. A move to homogenize products across the world has merely demonstrated that in many cases brands need differentiation even at a local level. It's no longer sufficient to be all things to all men. Brands need a strong personality; they need values and attitude; they need to attract a strong, even fanatical following to succeed. In the same way that pop groups have their devotees and fan clubs, brands need to develop a devoted fan base. This is only possible by clearly differentiating the brand. It may be that for every person who loves the brand another will dislike it. The point is that the fans will stick around.

3. FALL IN LOVE (``BRANDLOVE'')

Developing a strong brand personality will help engender a loyal brand following. But in itself it is not enough to ensure the sustained success of the brand, which must go further and wholeheartedly embrace the concepts that drive relationship marketing. A brand must woo consumers as a lover would. Once it has established what consumers desire, it must pander to their wishes. Over time they must build up a personal relationship, sharing beliefs and pursuing mutual interests. The relationship should be a two-way thing allowing for interaction. The idea is to create a relationship where parting is, as the bard says, ``such sweet sorrow.'' And if the bonds are sufficiently strong they may even give the brand a second chance if it makes an error of judgment that damages its brand equity.

Once the bond is created between brand and consumer, the challenge is to manage the relationship. Permission marketing is a variant on the relationship-marketing theme. The concept was developed by Seth Godin, who has honed his marketing skills at Yoyodyne (a company he founded) and then at Yahoo!. It relies on creating a relationship between company and consumer through the granting by the consumer of permission to take some form of action – to send product details, for example – in return for receiving something of value – a gift, say. The difficulty with permission-based relationships lies in keeping them alive – in other words, preventing the consumer from feeling that the permission has lapsed through lack of contact.

In the same way, whoever is responsible for a brand must nurture the bond with the consumer. The brand's implicit promise to the customer must not be broken by, for example, the brand straying too far from its core qualities. Extending a brand unnecessarily and inappropriately is a good way of straining a great relationship.

4. PUT A PRICE ON THE BRAND

The balance sheet was once the province of fixed assets such as machinery and property, earnings revenue, and other tangible assets. In the more enlightened business environment of the 1990s, corporations finally began to realize that there were other "soft" assets equally as important. Look as long as you want, but you won't find the value of the knowledge held in employees' heads reflected in a company's accounts.

The Aaker, Kelly, and Jacobsen study of the relationship between brand equity and stock price seems to suggest that there is a direct correlation between the two.[2] In the future, the value of a brand will inevitably find its way into the company accounts in one form or another. It is simply too valuable for it not to do so. Corporations must recognize that the brand is the company's Most Valuable Player and afford the brand the attention its status deserves.

5. MAKE YOUR BRAND A CORPORATE TOUCHSTONE

Brandlove between the consumer and brand is a desirable thing. Equally desirable is a good relationship between the brand and the workforce. A brand is a perfect instrument for focusing the efforts of employees.

First, a clear brand identity needs to be established. The brand needs to have its personality defined, its philosophy, its attributes. Once this is done, the brand can then act as a guiding light for behavior inside the corporation (and, it is to be hoped, outside as well). The brand can be used to galvanize employees. The company must be aware, however, that it cannot send out messages that conflict with the brand's identity.

In this way, the brand plays a role similar to that of corporate values where a company has expressly stated those values and uses them to align the company and its workforce. In the case of corporate brands, the brand values and the corporate values will of course be similar, if not identical. For companies that deal with a portfolio of products and that do not have a strong corporate identity, the alignment of company values and brand values is more difficult.

Ownership and attachment to the brand within the organization is critical to the brand's success. It needs long-term support from within the organization. Without it, the brand will be unable to develop its personality fully. Too often there is a tendency among brand managers to concentrate on the more superficial aspects of a brand, such as its image, in order to gain short-term hits. A successful brand will outlast many brand managers.

6. KNOW YOUR PLACE

The proliferation of niche markets and the corresponding fragmentation of mass markets mean that a brand has to know its place in the market to succeed. Focus is just as important in finding a brand's place in the market as it is in creating a brand identity.

Different markets require different expertise. In the case of product markets, increasingly this means having the necessary technological know-how and innovation. Branding a distribution channel requires an ability to forge alliances with other brands for the purposes of co-branding exercises. Expertise in creating brand experiences is an important skill where the branding of services is concerned. A company must know what it wants to do and where it wants to position itself in its industry. In an increasingly transparent world it is easy for a brand to be "found out" if it's operating in the wrong market.

7. GET CONTINUOUS FEEDBACK

To survive, a brand must continually improve. This is true in nearly all cases. There are some exceptions – Coca-Cola being one famous example – where the brand trades on traditional values and the consumer is unlikely to react kindly to change. There are few brands, however, that have sufficient brand equity to be able to shrug off continual improvement without eroding the added value they represent and giving ground to more innovative competitors.

The cornerstone for improving the brand is innovation; but brand innovation is not limited to the company. There is every reason why the consumer should be involved in the process. In fact, in a brand that has built brandlove and has a loyal following, consumers will want to get involved.

A great example of this is the computer games industry. Take the military strategy game *Command and Conquer: Red Alert. Command and Conquer* has been through a number of incarnations, each different from the last, each containing important modifications yet still retaining the essence of the brand and so not alienating fans. In part, game players have driven this modification and product-enhancement process. It is more than simple beta testing – a practice the computer software industry has carried out for some time now. Beta testing allows users of software to test it and report back on the errors they discover. Some might say that this is merely an exercise to cut R&D costs and is essentially corporate laziness. In the case of *Red Alert*, however, fans have built their own Internet Websites dedicated to the game and provide continual feedback to the game developers as to how they might improve the next version. For some computer games this feedback goes as far as writing original code and creating new levels for games.

This is a perfect example of how to harness the creativity of the end user to sustain brand equity.

8. FIND BRAND PARTNERS

When brands were a mass-market phenomenon, many had weak, immature brand personalities. Understandably, companies were reluctant to market their brand in tandem with that of another company, thinking, probably correctly, that there was a risk of diluting their own brand's identity.

The strategy of avoiding co-branding made sense then but makes little sense now. If a brand is built with a strong personality, there will be no question of it losing its identity in a co-branding exercise. Instead there is much to be gained by leveraging the brand to the maximum, and forging alliances that are consistent with the brand's identity. Alliances will, however, tend to be between brands with similar standing, as brand strategists will see little payback in associating with a weaker brand. The alliance between Coca-Cola and Nestlé to develop joint beverages is a good example of brands with rough parity forming a partnership. Exceptions to the equal-status rule might occur if the weaker brand offers certain credibility or value that would not normally be attainable. It might, for example, provide access to a trendy new niche market for a more traditional brand.

9. PROTECT YOUR BRAND

Counterfeiting of branded goods has been a serious problem for companies, especially in luxury goods markets. Corporations targeted by forgers usually pursue any breach of intellectual property rights ruthlessly through the courts. The issue of domain-name "cybersquatting" has also raised the profile of intellectual property rights, with some corporations trademarking generic terms associated with their brands.

Ultimately, however, it is not the law that is the real barrier to rogues selling fake goods to consumers. The real barrier is the added value and experience associated with the brand itself. Certainly near-perfect copies are likely to confuse the consumer. However, if the sum of the brand's attributes is greater than just the product or service, something that will have to be the case if it is to prosper in the modern business world, then no counterfeiter can provide the authentic brand experience. Assuming consumers know that they are buying fake goods, then they will weigh the cost saving against everything the real brand offers in terms of quality, experience, and other brand values. If the brand is sufficiently strong, these brand factors will outweigh cost savings. Purchasers of pirate software, for example, may save money, but they will be unable to receive all the benefits and value offered by the software brand through registration, such as software updates and help-desk backup.

10. NURTURE THE BRAND

Once a company has breathed life into its brand, it is not just a question of standing back and letting the brand get on with it. The brand's vital signs must be constantly monitored to ensure it is healthy and thriving. Frequent brand audits, brand tracking, and consumer research focus groups are all tools that may be used to keep the brand on track.

THE END OF THE BEGINNING

When Regis McKenna says "I don't think we can tell the difference any more between a corporate strategy and a marketing strategy", the world-famous marketing guru may truly believe that the end of marketing as a separate organizational function is upon us.[3] Or he may just be being provocative. The age of the brand, however, is far from over. What we are witnessing as we move into a new century is the struggle of brand strategists to keep pace with dramatic changes in the business world. Increasingly sophisticated consumers, increasingly transparent markets, and increasingly complex products and services will make tremendous demands on those responsible for brand development. Innovation and sensitivity are the key to surviving.

An innovative approach to branding means harnessing creativity to drive the brand forward, constantly improving it yet retaining its essence. It also means having an open mind and being receptive to new branding techniques – those, for example, developed by fledgling Internet companies seeking to stamp their brands on the world. Sensitivity means having a heightened awareness of consumers' response to the brand, to the brand personality, and to what else is happening in the marketplace.

Creating a great brand is a tough proposition in the modern business world. Adopting some of the ideas expressed above is a good starting point.

LEARNING POINTS

10 steps to making branding work:

» Own minds, not products.
» Dare to be different.
» Fall in love ("brandlove").
» Put a price on the brand.
» Make your brand a corporate touchstone.
» Know your place.
» Get continuous feedback.
» Find brand partners.
» Protect your brand.
» Nurture the brand.

NOTES

1 Gad, Thomas (2000) *4-D Branding*. Financial Times Prentice Hall, London.
2 Aaker, David A., Kelly, Michael Kelly, Jacobson, Robert. "Brand News". *Business 2.0* Website at www.business2.co.za/infront/ebusiness/124240.htm
3 *Business 2.00 Magazine*, Europe edn. December 2000.

Frequently Asked Questions (FAQs)

Q1: What is a brand?

A: See Chapter 2, Section: Defining brands and Box: Brand types.

Q2: What are the world's most valuable brands?

A: See Chapter 1, Table 1.1: The world's most valuable brands, 2000.

Q3: Who is responsible for brand development within an organization?

A: See Chapter 6, Section: Brand custodianship.

Q4: I want to create/sustain a brand. How do I go about it?

A: See Chapter 10, Ten steps to making branding work.

Q5: What does the term "corporate brand" mean, and why is it important?

A: See Chapter 6, Section: The rise of the corporate brand.

Q6: What is brand equity?

A: See Chapter 8, Section: Brand equity.

Q7: Is the process of creating a brand on the Internet different from traditional branding?

A: See Chapter 4, The e-dimension: E-branding.

Q8: What are good real-world examples of successful brands?

A: See Chapter 7, In practice: Branding success stories.

Q9: How do I find out more about the subject?

A: See Chapter 9, Resources.

Q10: What are the origins of modern branding?

A: See Chapter 3, The evolution of brands.

Acknowledgments

The author would like to extend his thanks and appreciation to: Des Dearlove and Stuart Crainer for their considerable assistance with researching and writing this text; the publishers of the *Express Exec* series, Capstone; and, last but not least, to Claire and Poppy for their patience and tolerance.

Index